THE
PILLARS
OF
EXCELLENCE

• • • • • • • • • •

A Peak Performance
&
Life Enhancement Course

• • • • • • • • • •

JOHN P. DEMANN, PH. D.

Bloomington, IN   Milton Keynes, UK
authorHOUSE™

AuthorHouse™
1663 Liberty Drive, Suite 200
Bloomington, IN 47403
www.authorhouse.com
Phone: 1-800-839-8640

AuthorHouse™ UK Ltd.
500 Avebury Boulevard
Central Milton Keynes, MK9 2BE
www.authorhouse.co.uk
Phone: 08001974150

First published by AuthorHouse 9/1/2006

ISBN: 1-4259-3908-2 (sc)

Library of Congress Control Number: 2006904476

Printed in the United States of America
Bloomington, Indiana

This book is printed on acid-free paper.

Visit Dr. John P. DeMann's website at:
www.pillarsofexcellence.com

This book is dedicated to my devoted wife Dana and my loving children Ricky and Carlie. It is with their love and support that I am able to pursue my life long dream of teaching and inspiring others.

CONTENTS

INTRODUCTION

In this book you will find a life enhancement technology that will change your life. The Pillars of Excellence program will give you the skills and guidance you need to overcome challenges, achieve your dreams, and attain fulfillment. The program will also guide you in developing motivation, drive, spirit, and purpose. You will attain extraordinary health, fitness, energy, and vitality. You will also develop the ability to gain true knowledge, wisdom, skill, and creativity. You will improve your emotional tones, therefore your productivity. This program will guide you to extraordinary communication by developing your affinity and reality with both living and nonliving entities. It will guide you to responsible, abundant, and consistent contribution. When you complete this program, you will know where you are going, why you are going there, and how you will get there. This book will guide you in developing a life of mastery, in which you will achieve what the Pillars of Excellence program refers to as Optimum. Optimum is a state of existence that requires certain actions to attain, but once you create Optimum, you will be able to accomplish anything you desire.

The Pillars of Excellence program is a peak performance and life enhancement course. Peak performers have certain characteristics, and this program will guide you in developing these characteristics so that you too can become a peak performer and enhance all areas of your life. If you are already a peak performer, the program will give you the ability to perform at even higher levels. My background as a peak performance coach has provided me with the experience and education to bring to you the latest technologies that will give you the extra advantage needed to perform above and beyond expectations. The Pillars of Excellence program is the foundation of peak performance and successful living. We all need to perform optimally whether we are at work, at home, or just enjoying life; and this program will give you the tools needed to live your life effectively.

Throughout my life I have always been interested in the concept of success and optimum performance. I searched high and low and read literally hundreds of books and studied any research material that had anything to do with self-improvement, performance, happiness, and fulfillment. I even earned a master's degree in psychology, and at the time of this writing I am currently working on my PhD and am writing my dissertation on optimum performance and life enhancement technologies and strategies. As you can see, my interest continues, and my life's work is committed to the development of the most effective self-help program ever created. I truly believe that I have found the most effective formula in the Pillars of Excellence program, and now I want to share it with as many people as possible.

My studies have led me to conclude that success literature today is much different than success literature of two hundred years ago. Earlier literature focused on character and development of the person from an inside-out approach. Today's success literature focuses on trying to change people by telling them how they should behave. This is an outside-in approach. True change comes from within a person, which requires an inside-out approach. Many of today's programs tell us how we should behave and try to get us to internalize an appropriate behavior for each individual situation. Trying to change another person's behavior by telling him or her how to behave is impossible, and even if it could work, why would we want it to work? Doing so would only create a world of robots in which everyone had the same personality--similar to that found in the movie The Stepford Wives. Our world is a wonderful place because of our different personalities. Also, telling others how to behave can never work, because doing so takes away the required ownership that is needed to consistently take any action. For anyone to consistently perform requires ownership, and the only way anyone can own anything is for the action or thing to be his or her own desire or idea. Our country and world are in a downward spiral, because we live in an environment of flaky, fake behavior that is caused by today's plastic approach to improvement. I believe it is time to change this approach and bring about real growth for personal development.

So many people waste their time and money on literature that promises overnight success but delivers only a fraction of what is expected. In some cases people have been injured emotionally with these snake oil approaches. In other cases people have been injured physically by following special diets and exercise programs that require them to go to an extreme for results. Having myself been a victim of the snake oil salesmen, I know how frustrating it can be to pick up a book or a program believing it will change your life and guide you to greater success, happiness, and fulfillment only to find another empty promise that ends up being a waste of time and money.

In my work I have come to recognize that for real change to occur it has to come from within. Many of us have witnessed or experienced the New Year's resolution or a goal that fails early in the process of attainment. This usually occurs because it is a resolution or goal that has been given to us from an outside source. For instance, your well-meaning wife says, "Honey, I really think you should lose about twenty-five pounds," so you resolve to lose weight. However, this is not truly your own resolution; it came from your wife, so you never owned it in the first place and are less likely to succeed. If we want to achieve something, we must have ownership in the goal if we are to take consistent action and experience positive results.

Since change can only come from within, the individual seeking change must become an active partner in determining what it is they want to change and how they want to change it. I believe the answers to life's questions lie within each and every one of us. It's important to note that for any consistent motivation, these answers can only come from the person who is seeking change. The Pillars of Excellence program can't make changes for you. However, it is designed as a guide to help you determine what is important in your life and to guide you in planning how you will attain the life you desire. It is an inside-out approach that can help you to find your purpose and create the natural motivation to attain the life you have always dreamed of.

Today we live in a world that presents us with a plethora of information, most of which is not necessary to complete the task of teaching a subject. I intentionally wrote this book in such a way that you are given only the information that is necessary for you to completely understand and grasp the topic. My main goal is to teach the material so that it is fully understood and so you will be able to use the information consistently. For this reason I have left out all the professional jargon that so many other books and programs use merely to impress the reader.

In order to get as much out of the program as possible, I am including some study tips to guide you in gaining the information you need to successfully implement the program. I have created a study technology that you will be given, in part, later in the book. You can also take the course, which is part of the Pillars of Excellence Life Improvement series, to get a full understanding of the study technology.

I would like to take a moment to explain that the reason I want to include these study tips is that when I was young I was diagnosed with dyslexia, but I did not have the typical symptoms of dyslexia. I knew something was wrong but had no idea what it was. I finally found the problem, which had nothing to do with dyslexia: I had no idea how to learn. In fact, I believe this is true for many people diagnosed with learning disabilities--they are being misdiagnosed. In my experience the problem lies not with some fancy label that only frustrates the student, but rather with learning skills.

The technology presented in this book teaches you how to learn, how to remember, and more important, how to use the knowledge you gain. You will find the study technology one of the most powerful tools you can ever use, because it gives you the ability to learn anything you want or need. In fact, I have helped many students who were once diagnosed with a learning disability. Once they were given the new skills that are taught in this program, they no longer showed signs of any learning disabilities. It's also important to note that when a child is given the label "learning disabled," he loses a great deal of self-confidence. In working with these students I have found that once they learn how to learn, they become more confident.

There are three basic reasons why we fail to understand the material we study. The first is that we often learn about a subject without having the actual object in front of us. In short, we are absent the physical mass of the object we are dealing with. For this reason I want to stress that you should always try to understand the subject in real life. Use it while you learn it. You can also try to create greater understanding by using a demo kit, which replaces the physical mass if you can't get the mass in front of you. A demo kit is made up of regular household objects like pencils, paper clips, rubber bands, and other similar objects that can, with a bit of imagination, represent those objects or concepts you are trying to learn. However, nothing is as good as the real thing, so try to introduce as much reality as you possibly can into your learning. For example, if you are learning about a certain car, it is best to be in the presence of the car. In the case of learning an abstract concept, like math, it is best to actually perform the actions--in this case addition, subtraction, multiplication, or division--as you learn. If it is not possible to study in front of the object, then use a demo kit that represents the part of the object you are studying. With regard to learning concepts, you can use the demo kit as a means to demonstrate your knowledge of the subject.

The second reason many people have trouble understanding a topic is because of the gradient of the learning curve. In other words, the material is presented either too quickly or too slowly for us to grasp. If the material is presented too quickly, we may have difficulty comprehending it. If it is presented too slowly, we tend to get bored and wander off the topic, again losing track of the material. This is one of the biggest problems in learning and is actually one of the reasons that so many people are diagnosed with learning disabilities. In other words, when a person is diagnosed with dyslexia, they often are not dyslexic; instead, material is being presented to them at such a slow pace that they get bored. This is also true of attention deficit disorder (ADD) cases, in which the individual has difficulty maintaining attention to a topic.

Of course there are many people who are truly learning disabled, but even in these cases the Pillars of Excellence study technology can be of significant help. There are a lot of great people helping those who are learning disabled, and I don't intend to take anything away from them; however, I'd like to suggest that we begin to look at new ways in dealing with this problem. Perhaps if people realized the devastating effect that the label "learning disabled" has on a person's self-esteem and overall confidence, they would be more compassionate toward those who have learning difficulties. There are many people--both children and adults--who have suffered this label and whose lives have subsequently been affected in negative ways as a result. If you are one of these people or know someone who is, the Pillars of Excellence study technology can be a life-changing tool in itself.

The third reason people fail to fully understand the material at hand is because they are unfamiliar with the vocabulary being used. You may have noticed this when you are reading and you get to the end of the page and realize that you have lost touch with what you just read. This happens because somewhere along the way you went past a word you did not understand. To help solve this problem, go back to a point you do understand, begin reading from there, and find the word you did not comprehend. Once you find the word, look it up in a dictionary and try to thoroughly teach yourself the word by familiarizing yourself with it enough so that you can use it correctly.

When reading, always keep a good dictionary by your side and look up words you are not sure of. In any study I would suggest that you first understand the basic vocabulary of the subject by prereading. Skim through the text page by page, circling the words that belong to the subject and learning them. At first this may take some time, but in the end you will shorten your learning time and increase your retention of the material.

With anything you learn, use it so that you can fully grasp it. Also, try to teach it to others. When we know we are going to teach what we learn to others, we instinctually put forth greater effort in trying to understand it. Another benefit to teaching the material is that teaching reinforces the material, which helps us internalize it more quickly. Nothing is more effective than using the material for its intent. This gives us the opportunity to truly understand it.

This book is set up in a step-by-step fashion, so it is important for you to read the book in the order in which it is presented. It is also important to take your time in working through the book, which includes practical exercises that will enhance your learning. The program was developed with the individual in mind, in that it allows you to create your own future. It is a life enhancement system that is personalized to fit your needs. Work the exercises in this program to completion, and I guarantee that your progress will be accelerated.

I'm not going to kid you and tell you that the work is going to be easy--it's not. In fact, this may be one of the most difficult and painful tasks you will ever have to do. I will not promise overnight success, but if you put forth true effort, you will experience extraordinary change in a reasonable amount of time. You will gain a sense of growth early in the program, and you may even experience a sense of fulfillment and greater happiness as soon as you start implementing the technology into your life. The Pillars of Excellence program can provide the stable basis you need to not only organize your life, but also make it more productive.

My main goal in life is beneficence. This means I love to help others grow and improve their life. Developing the Pillars of Excellence program and sharing it with the world is allowing me to live my life's purpose, which brings great fulfillment and meaning to me. I would like to thank you for giving me this opportunity to help guide you to greater meaning and fulfillment as well. Read this book, use what you learn, share it with a business associate, a friend, a loved one, or even a stranger, and enjoy the feeling you will attain when you see someone else making progress and living a more meaningful, productive, and fulfilling life. We are remembered for what we give, not what we take, so begin now by giving yourself the knowledge, wisdom, and skills that the Pillars of Excellence program has to offer. You too can begin a life of beneficence and help others grow, and together we can make this world a saner and more fulfilling place to live.

CHAPTER 1

A PREVIEW OF THE PILLARS OF EXCELLENCE PROGRAM

I once came across the following definition of the word "self-help": "the care or betterment of one's self by one's own efforts, as through study." This definition tells only part of a true self-help program. We could also add to this definition "as through action." The initial definition addresses only the theoretical part of study. A more complete definition should also include the use of what one learns. In other words, nothing is truly learned unless the knowledge gained can be used for its intent by the person learning it. Thus, the knowledge you gain in this self-help program must be put to use for its fruits to be realized.

The Pillars of Excellence program is not just any self-help program. It is a program that takes into account you, the individual, because you are the expert on your life. Many self-help programs today tell users of their program what they should do and how they should behave. However, for any goal to be achieved, that goal must be determined by the person who is trying to attain it, and this holds true as well with personal development. Where you go, in terms of growth, requires your input--you are the master and creator of the life you desire.

It is important to understand that the Pillars of Excellence approach offers you a basic structure from which to build your life so that you can realize your dreams and reach that pinnacle we call fulfillment. If we want to truly improve some aspect of our life, we must consider it with a holistic and balanced approach. For example, to maintain your car effectively, you must consider all of its parts. If you focus only on the engine, the car will not run optimally. However, if you maintain your car in a holistic and balanced fashion by considering all of its parts, the car will have a better chance to last longer and function more reliably. This also holds true for you, the person.

Many self-help programs direct your focus on just one or two parts of you. This is not true self-improvement, because you are not maintaining all of your parts. True growth comes from a holistic and balanced approach where all of your parts, as a human, are considered. The Pillars of Excellence program is based on seven specific core characteristics, or "parts," of man and will guide you not only in maintaining these parts, but also in developing and enhancing them further. The first three are the personal characteristics of man: spiritual, physical, and mental. The last four are the interpersonal characteristics, which allow you to interact more effectively with the world: emotional, social, service, and leadership.

By using this program to evaluate and fine-tune these seven characteristics, or pillars, within yourself you will develop extraordinary motivation, energy, and creativity. You will be in charge of your own emotional states and develop the integrity that is required in any relationship, including the most important one-- your relationship with yourself. You will be guided in contributing consistently and abundantly the gift you have to offer to the world. Finally, in its purest form you will know where you are going, why you are going there, and how you will get there.

To gain knowledge on any topic, a person should not have to bury himself in a text that offers only theoretical knowledge. True learning comes when knowledge gained is used for its intent, and this book provides a blend of information and suggestions for implementation that will help you internalize the knowledge and use it effectively. Please take your time in working through this course. Apply each aspect to your life in the order presented. When you have completed each pillar, not only will you understand that pillar theoretically, but also that pillar will begin to be a part of you. Within each pillar, you will know exactly what it is you desire, why you desire it, and how you can attain it.

The Pillars of Excellence brings to you a philosophy and a way of life that can enable you to experience life to its fullest. It can help to remove chaos and crisis from your life and bring to you a stable basis that can give you a better foundation on which to produce and live life more effectively. Be creative, and don't worry whether you can or cannot accomplish whatever it is that you desire. Simply try to bring out from within yourself the child who used to dream and live with a sense of hope and anticipation of better things to come.

Throughout my research in the area of human development, I have found that all people share similar characteristics but differ in personality. Most personal development programs focus on trying to change personality, but doing so will never work. Changing your personality would result in the creation of a new person. Your personality is who you are; it is the "I" of you. Personality, in other words, is "the person" in each and every one of us. To change the "I" of someone would require the replacement of the person, and this is literally impossible unless you believe we can switch from body to body. Our personality is what makes each of us unique and special.

Realizing that it would never work to change a person's personality in an effort to enhance life motivated me to think deeply about what people can do to improve their life. The first question I asked was, What is it that a person is trying to do when they approach the desire for change? Are they really trying to change the "I" of them? Do they really want to get rid of their own unique print?

When you think of the terms "self-improvement" and "self-help," these names suggest action upon one's self. "Improvement" and "help" are similar in that they both involve betterment of a person in a certain way. When someone is looking for improvement or help, he or she is seeking a way to change a behavior, improve a behavior, or take on a new behavior. For example, when a woman wants to lose weight, she is looking to improve her appearance and health. To do this, she has to change the way she behaves in her current lifestyle. She needs to change the way she eats and the way she moves. In other words, she needs to change her nutrition and exercise, not her personality.

Knowing that trying to change personality would only result in frustration and minimum improvement, if any, I began to think about what we all have in common as people. To improve something we must improve what exists. The next questions I asked myself were, What exactly is man made of? What is common that makes man, man? In other words, what are the parts of man that we can improve to improve life? Asking these questions moved me to develop the Pillars of Excellence.

Going back to the example of the automobile, every car has parts that make it perform, and these parts are basically the same in every car. For example, every car has wheels, an engine, a gas pedal, a brake pedal, and so on. If you take care of your car in balance, it will run optimally; however, if you do not take care of it, it will run less than optimally. Even if you maintain the engine and ignore the other parts of the car, the car may run a bit better than if you had not cared for it at all, but it will still not run optimally, as it would if you cared for the car holistically. Man is no different; we have common parts that make us human, that allow us to live, and if we care for these parts, we will perform optimally. However, if we do not take care of all our parts, we will experience a reduction in performance and a reduction in happiness.

The parts of man are common among all human beings. They see no difference regardless of race, religion, color, or culture. During my research I began to track common characteristics and found several that exist among all people. These characteristics were evident in both fulfilled and unfulfilled people. The difference was that those who were successful showed more developed characteristics than did the less successful people. In other words, successful people tend to focus on developing their seven core characteristics.

This raised another question: could it be that these characteristics are the key to personal development? The answer was obvious. YES! If a person wants to develop himself in any way, wouldn't it make sense to develop the whole person? The answer again is YES! Therefore, the key to any personal development program or organizational development program, which will be discussed later, is the understanding of these characteristics and their development.

Most successful people, if not all, have either consciously or unconsciously developed certain common characteristics. These characteristics hold the key to life enhancement and optimum performance. When we cultivate these characteristics, we train our abilities to function at higher levels, therefore enhancing our performance and productivity. It is in these characteristics that the Pillars of Excellence program was born, and it is in these pillars that you will experience extraordinary personal growth, including greater performance, productivity, and fulfillment.

As mentioned above, each individual is made up of seven characteristics, or what I refer to as "pillars": spiritual, physical, mental, emotional, social, service, and leadership. The first three characteristics are your personal characteristics; the last four are your interpersonal characteristics. The personal characteristics are those that support the individual on a personal level. The interpersonal characteristics are those that support the individual on an interpersonal level.

THE SPIRITUAL PILLAR

The spiritual characteristic is not reserved specifically for religion. Religion is a personal choice, and as I have explained, I don't intend to influence your ideas about religion in any way. When I speak of "spiritual" with regard to the Pillars of Excellence, I am speaking of the internal person. We all have a spirit, which can be labeled as the "I" of you. The Spiritual Pillar is that place where we define who we are. It is the place that gives us our driving force and our beliefs in terms of our ethics and morality. It is our belief system, where we define what this journey we call "life" is all about. We define our purpose within the Spiritual Pillar, and it is that purpose that gives our life meaning. A person's purpose is deeper than the definition of what he or she does, such as being a doctor, lawyer, or housewife, because it looks at something more important than a job or what kind of car we drive. Purpose is how one defines his or her principles.

The point is this: spirituality is where our belief structure is formed, and it is from here that we find the foundation for our motivation, drive, spirit, and purpose. In the Pillars of Excellence program you will be guided in developing your own belief system that matches what you profess to believe in. It is your guide to knowing who you are in the purist sense, and it is where you find your ability to live with purpose.

Once you know who you are--by defining your true beliefs and creating the character that matches those beliefs--you will be well on your way to developing the fuel for life. You will develop motivation, drive, spirit, and purpose. You will be motivated not just to survive, but to survive on top of the mountain. You will be driven to stand firm in your beliefs, and you will develop the character needed to live with others in harmony. You will be given the ability to find your purpose; therefore, you will be able to live with greater productivity and happiness.

THE PHYSICAL PILLAR

The Physical Pillar can be defined as your physical body. This includes your bones, muscles, organs, skin, hair, and any physical characteristics you have. It is that part of you that transports your spirit. It is what allows you to breathe, think, and pump blood; in short, it is the part that physically exists. The physical part of man can be either healthy or sick, which is very much dependent on how it is treated. If one does not care for their physical body, then they can expect to experience less than optimum health, energy, vitality, longevity, and a reduction in the quality of life.

The Pillars of Excellence program takes a balanced approach to caring for the physical characteristic of the person and operates with a prevention philosophy. This means that we approach our wellness from the belief that it is much more effective to prevent disease than it is to focus on the cure of disease. In the prevention approach we try to care for the whole person physically. The prevention philosophy also looks at the person's spiritual, physical, mental, emotional, social, service, and leadership characteristics.

A number of insurance companies are taking a prevention approach by offering discounted policies for not only those who take care of their physical characteristic, but also those who live a prevention lifestyle. These insurance companies are even paying for things such as gym memberships, nutritional supplements, and the like. The reason for these discounted policies is that it is much less expensive to prevent disease than it is to try to cure it.

The Physical Pillar will guide you to greater energy, vitality, longevity, and quality through anaerobic, aerobic, and flexibility movements. You are also guided in developing a sane way to nutrition and healthy lifestyle choices. In the program you will learn the importance of exercise, nutrition, lifestyle, and reducing stress. You will be guided to living a life of wellness that fits your desires and goals. You will learn to live with great effectiveness, and you will be able to be an example to others and make a difference for someone else. This is true contribution, because it is the most precious gift you could ever give--the gift of living.

THE MENTAL PILLAR

The last personal characteristic in the Pillars of Excellence program is what separates us from the animal world--our minds, or the Mental Pillar. Here we find our most powerful tool for living successfully. It is where we find the answers to life's challenges and solve the problems that life throws at us. Many people define knowledge as power. However, I believe that knowledge is only potential power. True power comes only when knowledge is put to use. Our brains are complicated in physical structure, but very basic in function. In other words, we do not need to know the inner workings of the brain in order to use it; however, we do need to know some basic procedures to use it effectively. In school we were never taught how to work our brains, and our brain did not come with an owner's manual. We never really learned how to use it except from an "automatic" standpoint.

In the Pillars of Excellence program you will be guided in developing your ability to use your brain effectively and with great precision. You will also be guided in the process of learning so that you will develop a strong memory and the ability to truly learn anything you want to learn. You will be given the formula to put knowledge to work for you and your fellow man. In short, you will learn how to gain knowledge, wisdom, skill, and creativity. Most important, you will be guided in taking your thoughts and turning them into reality, allowing your true potential to shine.

THE EMOTIONAL PILLAR

The first interpersonal characteristic addressed in the Pillars of Excellence program is the Emotional Pillar. Emotional intelligence is becoming more important today; in fact, it has become a key factor in the hiring of new employees in corporations around the world. It has been shown that those with high levels of emotional intelligence are more successful than those with just high IQs. Of course the best possible scenario is a balance between the two.

What is emotional intelligence? It is having self-awareness of your ability to manage your emotions, to motivate yourself, to evaluate other people's emotional tones, and to bring to others their desired emotional states. The Pillars of Excellence program will guide you in developing your emotional intelligence so that you can learn and understand your emotions and the emotions of others. You will be guided in emotion evaluation and state management. You will learn the GPA Life Cycle, which helps you develop your Goals, Purposes, and Actions to give you the ability to change state at will by using physiological and psychological skills that will allow you to improve your emotional tones and therefore your emotional intelligence.

THE SOCIAL PILLAR

The next interpersonal characteristic is the Social Pillar. Man is a social being; people generally like to be liked and want to be a part of something special. In our desire to be a part of something special, we sometimes inadvertently say and do things that are not good for others. We get caught up in being the hero and wanting to be the one who makes the difference in another person's life. This desire often backfires and may lead to more problems than solutions. Remember, for anyone to make a change in their life, they must desire the change for themselves, and for this to happen the idea has to come from within themselves.

If you really want to help others, it is best to guide them to their own desires and be there for support and facilitation--to be their coach and guide them through open-ended questions that allow them to expand their thoughts and ideas. Open-ended questions force us to think and to come up with creative ideas to fix, change, or make better those aspects of our life that mean a great deal to us. To help another often requires letting them help themselves; in fact, backing off and letting someone help himself is one of the greatest gifts you can give.

To be liked we must be trusted. To be trusted we must have good character, and as mentioned above, the Pillars of Excellence program will guide you in developing your character. Once we have established our character, we must make sure we know our rules--in other words, what we believe to be right or wrong. Our rules and our actions are closely connected; if we act in ways that are in line with our rules, there is a greater likelihood that others will trust us. It is important to note that integrity plays a big part in our ability to develop relationships. It is not so much what we believe in than it is whether we are consistent in actions that support our beliefs. In other words, people will like us even if we hold different opinions as long as our actions are in line with our own opinions. When we don't get along with others, it is usually because we lack trust in that person.

A person with integrity believes in certain rules and values and operates consistently from these rules and values. However, a person with integrity never forces their rules or value system on others. To be liked one must be trusted, and trust is a two-way street. If we can't trust someone or they can't trust us, the relationship will never grow. How do we build trust? Integrity! How do we gain integrity? We simply define our own rules and values, develop a code of conduct that reflects the rules and values we hold, and then live by that code consistently. The Pillars of Excellence program will guide you in defining your rules and values. From your rules and values, you can then develop a code of conduct from which you will automatically make decisions. In short, the Pillars of Excellence program will guide you in developing your personal and interpersonal characteristics, as well as integrity and trust, by guiding you through a process of values clarification, rules clarification, and the development of your code of conduct.

THE SERVICE PILLAR

The next interpersonal characteristic is the Service Pillar. As mentioned above, we all want to feel needed, and the most powerful way to do this is through the gift of giving. We all feel important when we can contribute; this is a need all humans have. It is an internalized characteristic that is motivated by selfish reasons. I argue that there is no selfless intention when it comes to giving. Try to find one and you will have trouble, because giving is a selfish act. We have all heard the saying that "the gift is in the giving."

When we give, even with the intention of doing good, we often give purely for selfish reasons. In other words, we focus more on the pleasure we will receive by giving the gift than we do on how much the gift will help the recipient. Government welfare programs are an example of how good intentions can often fail. Although such programs are truly needed by some, they can also lead to problems, mainly for those who are on the program for extended periods of time. When someone receives the "gift" of welfare, it is only natural to want to keep receiving it. In fact, "getting" can be like an addictive drug in that we tend to get used to or expect a certain level of getting. The reality is that welfare programs enable their recipients to become dependent on the programs rather than on themselves to support their families. And since such programs have their limits, some people are left without knowing what to do when their welfare benefits run out. In addition, many politicians are not genuinely concerned about those people who are on welfare; they are only concerned about getting votes. If they truly cared about welfare recipients, they would see the damage that results from giving people money they haven't earned for themselves--how it creates an addiction and sucks the life right out of its victims.

I learned the hard way that giving can wreck the life of another. I used to help one family at a time, and I would give them a great deal of money, thinking that it would help them. I thought I was doing what I was supposed to do--to give abundantly. But every person I helped eventually ended up worse off than when I first started helping them. Every one of them in a period of three to four months quit their job and no longer held employment. My good intentions enabled them to leave their jobs and become dependent on me for their income. In the beginning this angered me, so I would cut them off, which led to a lack of income and thus their being worse off than when I had first met them. This went on for several years until I figured out what I was doing wrong. I am not saying we should not help others by giving money; rather, I am saying that our gifts must have a specific, positive purpose. In my case it would have been better if I had paid for their continued education, or if I had motivated them to get back on their feet by setting a deadline for how long or under what conditions I would continue the gift. The point is this: when we give, we must be very careful not to just look at it from how it will affect us as givers; we must also consider how it will affect the receiver in the long run.

In the Pillars of Excellence program you will be guided in developing your ability to give to others in ways that keep them in the game of life and improve their chances of survival. The end result in your giving should be that the receiver is better off and is able to eventually help himself and in the future can help others as you helped him. You will learn that knowledge is one of the most powerful gifts you can give. Not only will you be able to see what your contributions are doing for others, but you will also receive the benefit that comes from giving: the feeling of contribution.

THE LEADERSHIP PILLAR

The final interpersonal characteristic is the Leadership Pillar. In the Pillars of Excellence program, leadership is much more than leading the masses. In order to lead the masses, one must first be a leader of his or her own life. The Pillars of Excellence program starts its leadership development with the most important form of leadership: you. In order to be free, we must be able to lead ourselves. If we depend on others to lead our lives for us, we are giving our freedom away. We are slaves to others' desires and wishes. When we leave our leadership on the table, we offer our lives to other people's dreams and desires.

Leadership is the characteristic that allows us to be truly alive, because it allows us to direct our own lives and create the life we wish to live. It allows us to envision the future and to see that future as if it already exists. It allows us to have the hope and faith that we will experience a progressively greater life even in times of trouble. When we are in control of our own lives, we create our own destiny.

The Pillars of Excellence program will guide you to character-centered leadership, in which you will live the life that you have created, one that is in line with your true beliefs. Since leadership is situational in nature, the program will guide you in developing the skills required to live with the situation at hand. It will guide you to motivation, vitality, and greater knowledge. It will teach you emotional intelligence and give you the skills needed to develop lasting relationships. It will guide you to completing the tasks at hand on time, in good quality, and in ways that help others. Finally, it is a leadership program that guides you in the most important kind of leadership--the leadership of your own life.

When we take control of our life, we take control of our future. Our future is one of two outcomes: the outcome of another person's goals or the outcome of our own goals. We have all set New Year's resolutions or goals that we can't seem to attain. There are several reasons for this. First, sometimes the goals we set are not our own; instead, they are the goals of others or of society. We do not own the goal if it is the wish of someone else. The Pillars of Excellence program helps you to set the goals you desire and never suggests goals for you, so the goals are truly your own. Another reason people fail in attaining their goals is that they don't know why they set them in the first place, and even if they do know why, they never made the why strong enough.

The third reason that people fail to achieve the goals they set is that they don't consistently take the actions that are necessary for attaining the goal. The Pillars of Excellence program will assist you in developing an action plan and the motivation to take those actions consistently. In the program you will use the GPA Goal-Setting technology, which will offer you the ability to choose your goals, develop the purpose for attaining the goals, and develop the action plan and take the consistent actions needed to overcome any obstacles along the way. With the Pillars of Excellence program you will achieve your goals, because the goals you set will truly be yours.

Now, let's begin the program that will guide you to be the true you and give you the life you have always dreamed of. Good luck, and may you always look for the best in life, where you can find your dreams and make them real.

CHAPTER 2

MOTIVATIONAL FACTORS

In order for any personal development program to be effective, it must contain information about motivation. If we develop an extraordinary plan that will shape our destiny but we lack the fuel to take action, the work in shaping that destiny will be a waste of time. In this chapter we will look at motivation and provide specific techniques to help you recognize and develop your motivation. Once we complete this important part of the program, you will then be ready to begin shaping your destiny, developing your purpose and bringing extraordinary meaning to your life.

Man has long searched for the answer to the question, Why do I exist? This question has been mulled over for thousands of years without much success in terms of the answer. When we search for the answer to a question that has plagued us for so long, we often think the answer must lie in some deep philosophical thought that Aristotle, Plato, or some other famous intellectual would have to create. The problem with such thinking is that we are looking in the wrong place for the answer. In fact, the answer to most questions can be found in the most basic solution. In other words, we tend to overlook the answer, thinking it is something more than what it actually is. If we look at this question from a basic standpoint, the answer will hit us right between the eyes.

Why does man exist? What is man's main purpose? The answer, I believe, is to survive. All man is doing is surviving. If you think about all of your actions, you'll see that somehow they all lead to the desired result of survival. Some may ask the question, Why do we self-destruct? Why do we do things that hurt or even destroy our survival? In our makeup we have been given the triggers for survival, which we will discuss in detail later. For now, however, let's take a brief look at what these triggers are. Once you understand the triggers, you will see why we often self-destruct. The two forces that drive us to survive are the two forces of pain and pleasure. Pain and pleasure drive our behavior: we avoid pain and we seek pleasure. These two powerful triggers are extremely effective in accomplishing what they were designed to do, but man has created some problems that allow these two forces to operate against their specific purpose.

Pain and pleasure, when they work the way they are supposed to, are very effective, because they motivate us to avoid pain and seek pleasure. Pleasures, under normal circumstances, inspire us to seek healthy survival activities. In other words, the pleasure states we desire are created by survival behavior. The behavior causes a reaction that creates the desired pleasure. Sex is one example. We are driven to have sex because it is pleasurable, and sex leads to survival of not only one person's bloodline, but of all mankind.

Pain drives us away from nonsurvival activity. For example, guilt is a pain that most of us try to avoid. When we act in ways against natural principle, we experience pain by feeling guilty. More examples of pain and pleasure activities will be discussed in the next chapter, but for now I think you get the picture.

Like the rest of our bodies, our pain and pleasure triggers are chemically structured. When we are involved in activities that give us pain--for example, touching a hot stove or cutting a finger with a knife--a chemical reaction takes place that creates the sensation of pain. When we are involved in activities that create pleasure--sex or exercise, for example--the pleasure is caused by a chemical reaction that produces chemicals that make us feel good. One of these pleasure chemicals is endorphins. Endorphins are released for many reasons, one of which is physical activity. When we exercise, we produce endorphins that create in us a pleasurable sensation. This pleasure is often referred to as the "runner's high." Although our body may initially feel pain, our mind knows that exercise is good for us, so we are able to endure great amounts of pain to get the high we are after with the endorphin release.

Endorphins are also released psychologically. When we are involved in activities that allow for our personal growth, we promote the release of endorphins. One example of this is completing a list of tasks. Have you ever made a to-do list of all the activities you wanted to accomplish on a given day? When you completed the tasks you checked them off or crossed them out. This action causes the body to release endorphins and makes you feel good. Have you ever completed a task that was not on the list, but when you did the task you put it on the list only to check it off immediately? This is an example of your subconscious desire to feel the pleasure rush you receive when you complete work and cross it off. I have read studies that show that checking off a task that has been completed causes the release of endorphins, which gives us the pleasure state.

Unfortunately, man has been able to alter this natural pain/pleasure structure by creating chemicals that disrupt it. Recreational drugs are a good example. The reason people take drugs is to change either their physical or emotional state of being. They are looking for ways to feel good, and in the short term drugs are very effective for providing such feelings. Drugs were not produced for this reason, but when they are taken for the purpose of inducing a synthetic high, severe problems can result.

One of the problems experienced by those who take recreational drugs is the body's natural reaction to regulate the amount of the chemical in the body via receptor sites. These receptor sites shut off production of the good, natural chemicals that are present. For example, if a person ingested cocaine, his body would react by limiting or shutting off altogether the dopamine that cocaine simulates. Now the person has only the cocaine feeding the body, which has literally replaced the dopamine. When the cocaine runs out, the person is left without the dopamine and may become severely ill. The person literally needs the drug to feel normal, and the only way to feel normal is for his body to produce dopamine or for him to ingest more cocaine.

In the short run, the body will not produce dopamine, and the person must either endure the illness or take more of the synthetic drug that shut off the dopamine in the first place. When our bodies stop producing the natural endorphins or other natural chemicals that are replaced by synthetic drugs, there is a need to get that feeling again, and the only way to do it, in the short term, is to ingest the drugs that shut off your own supply. From here you get a full-blown dependency or addiction. In short, when we take a substance that causes pleasure but ultimately causes pain, we are not allowing our bodies to do the work. Instead, we are doing it ourselves, and in the end we increase our probability of death.

When we remove the body's ability to function on its own, we are enslaving our body and killing its spirit to live. Spiritual existence is a desire to survive as long as possible. When we look at the spirit of man, we often see religions promising eternal life in exchange for certain beliefs and behaviors that create the character of the religion. Character is the person's ability to act in ways that are in line with their beliefs. We will discuss this in detail in the chapter on the Spiritual Pillar. For now let us look at religion and its quest.

Religions seek to find ways to extend life. They often talk of eternal life, which gives us a solution to death. We do not want to die, so we cling to the hope that our religious belief will keep us alive forever in some way, shape, or form. I am not discarding religion as a legitimate practice. It's only natural to want to survive forever. We want to survive with such tenacity that we are willing to do whatever it takes to live forever. In religion, then, spirituality is selling us the ability to extend life beyond the life of our physical body.

Spirituality is very personal and is not the same as the Spiritual Pillar. Spirituality is a quest for eternal life. If we ignore this aspect, how can we survive beyond this life and into the next? This may sound mystical, but there is some reality to the fact that we desire to survive on two plains: the physical and the spiritual. We need to cultivate our spiritual desire to survive if we want to live a fulfilling life.

Survival exists on many different levels. Eight different levels of survival must be recognized if you want to use motivation to your advantage and if you want to explain behavior. The first, of course, is the survival of self. This is the most important to each of us, unless we have children, in which case the survival of their existence is more important than our own. It is important to note that survival of self has to be first in any situation that requires your existence, so it is accurate to say that survival of self is generally the most important level of survival.

The next level is procreation and the nurturing of children. We want our bloodline to keep going. This is deeply ingrained in us and is the primary reason for our natural sex drive. It is also a survival aspect for all of mankind and is one of the reasons there are more women than men.

The next level of survival is for the group. This is often seen in the family unit, where blood is thicker than water. Sicilian families are typically strong in this aspect because of their past and the requirement to be together for survival. We also see a desire for group survival in teams and the spirit that exists between team members. If you ever have a problem getting team players to work together, give them a reason to protect one another and you will have your unity.

The next level of survival comes when we are motivated to protect the survival of mankind. One example of this is how the world community continually struggles to find cures for disease. It was also seen most recently in the December 2004 tsunami in

Southeast Asia, which left nearly three hundred thousand people dead. People from all around the world helped in the relief. It was all done for the survival of mankind.

We are also motivated for the survival of all living things. Not only do we care about the survival of humans, but many of us are also concerned with protecting the animal kingdom, especially those species that are quickly becoming extinct. We see this motivation when a little boy has a problem killing an ant, or when we feel bad because we hit a squirrel with our car. Deep down inside we know that the survival of all living things is important.

Next on the scale of survival we see the survival of nonliving things, including matter, energy, space, and time. All of these entities are nonliving, but we nevertheless want to protect them. For example, we value time and wish there were more of it. Those of us who must meet deadlines often do whatever we can to avoid wasting time.

Another level of survival is the survival of spirit. Many people attend church services or live with a set of beliefs that they will defend. Some may even die for these beliefs. When someone seeks to find purpose or meaning in their life, they are protecting the survival of spirit. An example of this is found in a book by Viktor Frankl called Man's Search for Meaning. The book tells the tale of how meaning can keep us alive. Its setting is in a death camp of Nazi Germany where Viktor Frankl developed what he calls logotherapy. He could not figure out why only one in twenty-five prisoners survived the camp until he noticed that those who survived were those who gave meaning to their suffering. This meaning gave them purpose, and it is in this purpose that their spirit was able to survive. He tells a tale that describes how as he was being tortured, he realized that his captors were actually the ones who lost their freedom, because they hadn't found meaning in their lives as he had. He realized that although they could hurt his body, they could never drain his spirit. His intent was to show how his captors had no choice; they were performing a task just as automatons perform theirs.

The last motivation for survival is the survival of a creator. This does not have to be God per se, but it has to be something greater than self, because having a sense that everything in the world was created by one creator allows societies to get along. Even if various ideas of the creator exist, this unity of belief allows us to function together as a group and live in harmony. Earlier I mentioned that the survival characteristics of self, procreation/nurturing, the group, mankind, all living things, all nonliving things, spirit, and God or your creator were hierarchical in nature. This is true, but the true strength in the survival dynamic lies in the greatest number of dynamics that are protected. Here we are talking about giving your own life for the survival of other entities as long as you believe they are more important then your own existence or if the loss of your life is less than the loss of others--for example, putting your children's lives before your own. In war people are willing to die because they know that their death may save many more lives. This is the only reason there are loyalties in war and why others will die for their leader. But these people are not truly dying for their leader; they are dying for the nation. If it were only the leader asking, no one would go to war for him except perhaps his parents or significant other.

With regard to you and the choices and decisions you make, this dynamic survival scale can be a great tool in creating the right choices. Whenever you are faced with a decision, think of the eight survival dynamics and find the answer that saves the greatest number of them as you can, and you will find your answer. There are going to be times when you have to sacrifice a dynamic or two, but the best solution is the one that will allow the greatest number of dynamics to be protected.

Motivation comes from many things, and often we find it in things that do not originate in any type of survival. Today many people are driven by things that are not that motivating at all. They may motivate, but they motivate for shallow reasons, which creates a short-term form of motivation. The individual is off and running, trying to find that next thing that will drive them once the first motivating factor wears off. Some people are motivated by guilt. With guilt a person is manipulated by memories and the past, which becomes that person's driving force. When this happens the person becomes a prisoner of the past and doesn't live life for today. Living by guilt is also very unhealthy, and stress often becomes a major symptom.

Motivation comes in many forms, and it is important to understand what motivates you. Many people seek only pleasure, which creates a plethora of problems. Our society is stepping further away from delay of gratification, with many people concerned only with attaining immediate pleasure. For example, many of our financial responsibilities are put off for the attainment of a desire we can't afford by using the pay-later programs that most financial institutions offer, such as home equity loans. If a person is using these programs, you can bet they are delaying pain in other areas of their life as well. These delayed pains began to stack up, and eventually no amount of pleasure will be able to overcome the pain that has been delayed. Many of our mental illnesses, like depression, are the result of this kind of behavior. If we want to attain a driving force that will fulfill our desires, we need to consider survival and the triggers of pain and pleasure.

At the beginning of this chapter we looked at a question that has been on man's mind since his intellectual existence: what is man's purpose? As I said, to answer this we must understand the reasons for our behaviors. Again, many of our actions are acts to improve survival on several levels, and we are triggered to those actions through pain and pleasure. Remember, we can either be controlled automatically, or we can take control of our lives and create a life of mastery. Live the life you want to live, and never allow mediocrity to peck its ugly head around the corner. Get rid of those forces that control you, and life will be much more manageable. Control pain and pleasure instead of letting pain and pleasure control you. If you do this, your life will be in your hands, and you will be able to direct your actions and have the power to shape your destiny.

CHAPTER 3

THE SPIRITUAL PILLAR

A popular dictionary defines the word "spiritual" as "of, relating to, or affecting the human spirit or soul as opposed to material or physical things." To further understand the word "spiritual" we must also define "spirit," which the dictionary defines as: "the nonphysical part of a person that is the seat of emotions and character." It also says, "those qualities regarded as forming the definitive or typical elements in the character of a person, nation or group or in the thought and attitudes of a particular period."

We know from the definition above that being spiritual means being nonmaterial and that a person's spirituality is regarded as the part that reflects character. "Character" is defined as "the mental and moral qualities distinctive to an individual." This definition can also apply to a group in which mental and moral qualities are shared--for example, religion.

The Spiritual Pillar involves your beliefs and what you maintain to be your purpose. Your beliefs create your purpose, the driving force that motivates you to do what you do. For example, if you believe in treating others the way you want to be treated, then you will be motivated to avoid being part of any activity that would go against this belief. When we hold a set of beliefs, we are better able to develop an idea of the purpose of our life. For example, if you hold Christian beliefs to their purist form, you may then be motivated to bring others to God. In fact, all of your activities would be motivated for that outcome. If on the other hand you hold conflicting beliefs, or you are not particularly strong in a belief, which means you don't genuinely hold that belief, you will be driven to confusion in your actions, which will then be inconsistent. This inconsistency will show up in your character. It is your character that reveals your true beliefs and your true personality.

We must consider action, since action is the point at which our character is best revealed. Our actions speak of our true intent, and in order to maintain the reputation of possessing a good character, those actions must consistently reflect what we say and believe. When we violate a belief through our actions, we damage our own image of ourselves, which leads to low self-esteem.

In many cultures a person's beliefs determine his or her acceptance. If you do not hold the same beliefs as the rest of the group, you may be excluded from that group. This is why religion must remain a personal venture in any society, because it is common for groups to judge based on the beliefs of its members. Most religions or spiritual groups have similar laws that reflect that group's stance on right and wrong. In general, most people hold the same belief in terms of right and wrong. For example, in the Buddhist religion it is believed that harming another is wrong. This belief is also held in many other religions, and the difference comes only from the source of the beliefs. The point is this: most humans hold the same general laws in terms of acceptable behavior with a little twist here and there. This is important for us to understand so that we can accept others no matter where their beliefs come from. It gives us the ability to understand that we are all very much alike and that we all hold general laws that are accepted.

Where problems arise is when one individual or group violates another individual or group because that group or individual gets their beliefs from a different source. If you look at the general principles of most individuals or groups, you will notice that they reflect the same laws or beliefs in terms of behavior. When we start judging others based on their source of beliefs, we run into the problem of violating not only the beliefs of the other but our own beliefs as well. This type of behavior generally comes from extremists, who look at the beliefs with a fine-tooth comb and find the only difference to be that of source. These extremists cannot accept any differences, even though the outcomes are the same, so they treat the other group or individual as outcasts and violate their own general laws. They thus show their true character. We say we believe in not judging others, yet we judge others based on the source of their beliefs.

This is where most people get into trouble with regard to their understanding of their own beliefs, because it leads them to violate their beliefs and in turn generate low self-esteem. Also, when a person goes against their own beliefs, they have no solid footing to work from in terms of purpose. The purpose is lost because deep down inside they know their true nature; therefore, they hold no connection to what they claim to believe. Since no connection exists, they lose a sense of purpose and start to wander in terms of behavior.

To develop any spiritual base, one must have faith in what one believes. Faith is belief at its strongest. Believing in something that you have never seen or have never accomplished requires faith to accept it as a possibility or truth. If you believe you can make a million dollars a year but have never made that much money in that period of time, let alone in your whole life, you must have faith that you can attain this goal if you are even going to attempt it.

Our beliefs are often wrong in terms of our abilities. Many people believe they can't do something only because someone else has told them that they can't. Since they haven't given themselves a chance at the activity, they don't have the opportunity to learn who they are and are kept from realizing their dreams and desires. If on the other hand you are given the support that says you can do anything you want to do and you truly believe this, you will reach further and attain more of your dreams. Believing that you can do something gives you a sense of purpose in that it drives you to attempt the attainment of the desired thing. When you know you can achieve a desire, you are more likely to attempt the attainment of that desire. Research shows that if you are given the confidence, you will be more willing to try attaining an outcome. In fact, if you are certain you will reach a particular desired outcome, you will tend to reach for an even greater outcome that will challenge you even more. This challenge enhances your purpose and drive so you will be more consistent in attaining the goals you set. On the other side, if you are given a set of beliefs that do not match your true potential, you may never try to reach and stretch your abilities.

With this in mind, it is important to evaluate your beliefs and determine if they are in fact your true beliefs. List all of your beliefs and question them. See if they match your true potential. You may be surprised. When people believe that their abilities are lower then they really are, it prevents them from reaching their true potential. Remember when I said the main conflict between religions is not the beliefs themselves but the source of those beliefs? The same idea holds true with your personal beliefs. You have been given a set of beliefs not only from your experience, but also from the experience of those who influence you. For example, if other people have often told you that you're not very intelligent, you are very likely to believe that is true, even if it's not!

Let us look at some general beliefs and try to see if you can incorporate them into your belief system. One belief many people fail to have is I can accomplish anything I put my mind to. Another is I am smart enough to become whatever I desire to become. These are only two of many positive beliefs that you can incorporate into your belief system. The best way to do this is to start dreaming again of the life you desire and ask yourself whether you have the ability to attain that life. Be honest and list the reasons why you can or can't attain the dream. You will find that those reasons that say you can't really do not have any backing to them. Try to find the source of those beliefs, and I bet you will see that the belief came from someone who influenced you, such as a parent or mentor. When you begin to realize that it is not your own belief, tell yourself that you are not going to accept that belief any longer.

List all the beliefs you hold and determine if they are negative or positive. Separate the beliefs into two columns, then go to the negative ones and ask why you believe them. Take a good look at those beliefs, and try to determine if they are truly justified. Now look at the positive beliefs and ask yourself why you think they are true. Again, you will be surprised to find that the negative beliefs usually come from other people or from a failed experience; the positive beliefs are a result of successful experiences or positive support. Usually the beliefs you hold to be true are those that come from experience. This is why it is important to understand that even if you think you cannot achieve a certain goal, you still should try to justify its truth.

List ten new beliefs that you can incorporate into your life. These beliefs must be positive beliefs. If you come to one you are not sure of, write it in the positive column. I promise you can support that belief. If you have held a belief that did not come true--for example, you believed that you could finish a marathon but failed to complete it-- it does not mean that you are not capable of completing a marathon. It only means that you could not complete that particular marathon. The point is that even the experiences you have gained with certain beliefs are only that--experience. You can hold the belief If I fail, I will continue until I succeed. This belief will wash out the belief that you can't complete a marathon, and it will give you the drive and purpose to complete one.

Take the ten positive beliefs you listed and add them to the positive beliefs you previously held. Try to internalize them by reviewing the list and reminding yourself why these beliefs are true for you. Do this every day. Most important, test those beliefs as often as you can. When you use them, they will be ingested much faster and you will internalize them sooner. Take the negative beliefs, and review your reasons why they are not true. Do this every day until you understand that they are not true and are able to let go of them. Prove that such negative beliefs are false by going against them, but remember, you must get yourself to believe that you can do so. There is some truth to the saying that you can achieve what you believe. This is a belief in itself and can help you rid yourself of the negative beliefs you hold.

You may remember the gymnast who broke her foot on a vault and came back minutes later to win the gold medal by performing a perfect vault. She believed she could do it when she could have easily given up without anyone judging her. She had the perfect excuse, but she refused to believe that the games were over for her. She knew that if she could just complete that one last vault, she could achieve the dream of her life. By putting the negative belief behind her and carrying the positive belief within, she achieved one of the greatest feats ever in sports history. You too can accomplish much, even in the face of adversity. By fine-tuning your beliefs, your dreams can come true.

The Spiritual Pillar also reflects the "I" of you. Your personality is your spirit. It is your spirit revealing itself and is what makes you who you are. When you hold certain beliefs and know the purpose of your life, you automatically express it through your personality. We have all had to deal with people who seem to have a negative personality, or what is known as an antisocial personality, and at times you yourself may have acted in such a manner. It is revealed through the "I" of the person. We can hold a positive personality or we can hold a negative one. What determines whether you are generally a positive or negative person is based solely on your beliefs. If, for example, you hold the belief that all businessmen are greedy, then you will prejudge all businessmen and consider them to be greedy. This will bring out of you, through your personality, a negative belief and will in turn reflect your true character.

Once you understand the idea that your personality is not your physical body, you can recognize the meaning of true love and acceptance. When we first meet others, we often judge by appearance. But prejudging by appearance can be misleading. As they say, "You can't judge a book by its cover." It is difficult not to judge others by their appearance--first appearances do count for something--but until you actually know the person, you can't make a true evaluation of the person. For example, you may meet someone who has bad breath. Your first impression is to think that the person does not brush their teeth. What if that person is on some type of medication or has a physical condition that affects their breath? Now would this change your belief?

Here's another example: Joe was riding on a subway and encountered a man with two kids who were acting out of control. Joe's initial thought was that the man was not a good parent since he was allowing his kids to jump wildly around the subway car. Without thinking, Joe turned to the father and said, "You should really get your kids under control! They're bothering everyone on the train." The man quietly looked at Joe and told him he had just left the hospital, where he lost his wife after a long battle with cancer. Of course, the kids also lost their mother, and he just couldn't seem to get them to understand. The man was not in the state to care for them as he normally did. Joe felt terrible and, after offering his condolences, apologized for criticizing the man's children. This is an example of a paradigm shift, an experience we have after we know the whole truth. Thus, we should try to understand people as a whole, not just based on our first impression. The true person is inside the body, and only when you meet that part of the person can you make an accurate judgment of them. Since our beliefs can skew our judgments, it is important to remember that the only way to get an accurate assessment of a person is to open your eyes to the whole person and their circumstances.

We each hold a unique personality, and it is in this personality that we find the color of the person. Most self-help programs try to change the personality by trying to change the behavior by telling someone how to behave. This can never work, and it is why most self-help programs fail. Changing a person's personality would require that the person become someone else. We see this in multiple personality disorders, in which the personalities are separate from each other and the individual does not know of the other personalities. In fact, the person or persons are separate within the multiple personality, and they often ignore each other, not even knowing the other exists.

You can't help someone grow by telling them how to behave. It is easy to tell someone to quit smoking, but until that person holds the belief that they must quit smoking, nothing will happen. They may quit, but if they do not truly hold the belief that they must quit, they will eventually start smoking again. What does this have to do with personality? In general it says that a personality is that part of you that controls the direction of you. In other words, your personality directs your brain and guides your behavior. It is what you believe that creates the final touch to your personality, which then generates the production of you and your actions.

Having spirit, then, is having the knowledge of knowing that you are who you are. When you had spirit week in high school, you were encouraged to believe that you could win the game. It got everyone involved by getting them to believe that without the support of each and every one of them the end result would be failure. This is also apparent in the corporate world, where you can get a sense of the a company's general spirit in its culture. If the company is diseased, you will see distrust and a lack of spirit. On the other hand, other companies exist that carry a very clear spirit that says they are a good place to work. For example, the spirit of Southwest Airlines gives people the true impression that they are a fun airline to work with. The culture is clear and it generates trust. No one is going to hurt the other guy to get his or her job. Employees of the airline hold a set of beliefs that are in line with natural law, and they have internalized these beliefs, so the spirit is filled with the company culture.

Another example of how spirit works can be found in companies where workers have formed a union. In many cases, the company invited the union by treating the employees as equipment. The company's management gave employees the idea that they are there for one purpose and that is to serve the company, and anything outside of that is out of limits. Your kid gets sick and the boss says, "Get back to work." This mentality breeds a sick spirit. No one wants to be associated with this culture, so you see a great increase in absenteeism and other symptoms of the problem. The trust does not exist, and this is why it is next to impossible to change the spirit if the change does not include a shift in beliefs. If a company wants to get rid of a union, all they have to do is internalize a new set of beliefs that are in line with natural law and give the employee more pleasure without the union. This does not require more money; in fact, money will only cause greater resentment. Once the person feels as though he or she has been recognized as an individual, they begin to act in more responsible ways and their true nature will shine.

It is interesting to watch companies blame their employees for the loss in revenue when in fact the basic problem lies with the general spirit of the company itself. Change the spirit, and you change the culture. Eventually the union is no longer needed to protect the employee, and it now becomes a working part of the organization that helps it to increase profits. For a company to succeed, its management must recognize the spirit of man. The leaders must also understand that the company also holds a personality that disseminates its influence among the group; which means if the personality of the company is flawed, the company is flawed throughout.

Some companies have multiple personalities. In such companies the organization is working separately from each department. Employees are misdirected, as no one knows what is expected. This is a big reason many companies fail. The leaders of the company are responsible to disseminate the belief system. They are also responsible for the development of the company's personality. If this personality is supported by negative beliefs, it will emanate from it a negative attitude. If, however, the company supports and disseminates positive beliefs, then the personality of the company will generate a positive attitude.

Here's an example: at Company A the CEO told an employee that his family comes first, and if he was needed at home he should be at home. Company B's CEO told his employee that his job comes first, because it supports his family. Company A recognizes that family is first and that employees are people. The result is that Company A has loyal, hard-working employees. It is also a more profitable company, as with Southwest Airlines. The message sent by Company B, however, is that the employees do not matter. The difference between the two companies is like night and day. Company A has higher profits, lower costs in terms of employee pay and other areas, and lower absenteeism. Company B has lower profits, higher employee costs, and higher absenteeism. The point is this: if you want to be successful as an individual or as a company, you must hold beliefs that are accepted in terms of natural law, and you must understand the reality of the difference between the physical and spiritual aspects. The personality of individuals or groups who hold positive beliefs that are in line with natural law are healthier, happier, and more productive.

The ultimate goal in all of this is a connection with the physical aspect of the world and the personality or spirit of the person or the organization. When we connect, the outcome is the control of the environment, which leads to greater effect on the desired outcomes. When we experience disconnect, we see a loss of control of the environment, and the result is chaos. When we are in touch with ourselves, in terms of spirit, we reduce the crisis potential. When we experience crisis, it is because we have lost control of our spiritual being. We start to react and set off greater chaos. The situation tends to snowball, and soon the individual or the organization is in a downward spiral, headed toward death.

The true you will surface sooner or later, so today's self-help programs are destined to fail. You can't fake it--your personality is real, and it will reveal the truth of who you truly are. If you choose to influence others in plastic ways, by trying to be someone you are not, the end result will always be negative. If you try to act in certain ways in given situations, you will eventually slip and the true you will surface. Be yourself by defining who you really are. Understand your beliefs and accept the source of other people's beliefs. Feed your personality with beliefs that you can support, and you will begin to see a character emerge that is in line with truth. You will not have to fake it; therefore, your behavior will come naturally. You will be consistent, and you will learn to trust yourself. Your self-esteem will soar and so will your confidence. You will no longer have to run from yourself, and you will accept yourself for who you really are. Have fun getting to know yourself and building the most important relationship of your life--that is, the relationship between you and your beliefs.

Once you understand and are in tune with your beliefs, you will notice a greater sense of clarity. This is because you are more in touch with yourself, and you know what you do and do not like. You have gotten in touch with the real you. From here you will begin to notice a driving force that can give you the push to achieve something special. This force is such a powerful tool that without it nothing is possible. In fact, when people lose it they end up dead spiritually and emotionally.

What is this tool that is so powerful? It's purpose. Life without a purpose is a life of complete emptiness. When someone says they are depressed, lack of purpose is the problem, because their life has no meaning. It leads some people to commit suicide when purpose is absent. Purpose is the first key to any life worth living. Find your purpose and you have solved 99 percent of the equation. Maybe not 99 percent, but a great deal has been achieved when you find your purpose.

Many people know this truth, but they still seem to have a problem defining their purpose. One reason this happens is because they are waiting for someone else to tell them what that purpose is. If you want to know your purpose, you must ask yourself questions that direct you to finding that purpose.

Some people may claim their purpose comes from God, and this is true to some extent. Your purpose can come from your creator or from any source you believe in, but it is up to you to recognize your purpose when it reveals itself. The best place to start in finding your purpose is by examining your beliefs, desires, abilities, and--most important--your experiences. Often we fail in finding our purpose because we are not actively looking for it in the right places. Look at Lance Armstrong. Here is a guy who was given a death sentence, but refused to accept that outcome. I believe he has lived because his life began to have a very powerful purpose from his experience with cancer. In fact, he now believes he was given the disease so that he could give hope and show others that they do not have to accept cancer as a death warrant. When we look at our experiences, we find our expertise, and this is usually a place to begin looking for your meaning in life.

You can begin to find your purpose by asking yourself: What do I love doing? What do I enjoy doing? What do I value? Another question one should ask is, What am I good at? To get this answer just think about what others have told you what you are good at. However, keep in mind that if you are not good at something, this should not be the final indicator of whether you should do it or not. I believe if we have a strong desire to do something, we have the ability to do it--no matter what. We can always improve and get better at whatever we want to do. Of course, there are some limitations, but in most cases we can overcome lack of ability. We must be realistic and recognize our true potential. I have seen many people waste their life chasing a dream they can never achieve. It is better to have confidence, but be honest and real and look for the purpose of your life, not Tom Cruise's life.

A great way to find your purpose is to make a list of all your talents, desires, and the positive comments people have made about you. Here we can use a process of elimination. Eventually you will come across the purpose of your life. Another way, and probably the best way, to find your purpose is by examining your experiences.

If you want someone to perform a certain task, you usually choose someone with the appropriate experience, right? The same holds true for any activity: review what you have experienced in life, and your purpose may be peeking around the corner at you. The experiences that best reveal your purpose are those that presented the most challenge in your life. For example, the founder of MADD (Mothers Against Drunk Drivers) was the mother of a child who was killed by a drunk driver. Many people would give up after such a devastating loss, but for some it is the starting point of a life filled with purpose. If you yourself have suffered a tragic loss, look at the loss and try to determine if there is anything you can do with your experience to help others who are in the same situation. Life sometimes puts our purpose right in front of us, but sometimes we have to put forth a great deal of effort to find it. Become aware and start to look for your true purpose, and you will be able to add a great deal of meaning and fulfillment to your life.

One more point about finding your purpose. You must realize that your purpose may not be the same throughout your life. In fact, it may change several times, so you must try to recognize when a reevaluation of your purpose is required. The point is to always keep your eyes and ears open for a change in your purpose. Look for it daily in your experiences, compliments, abilities, and desires. You will find it, and when you do, your life will never be the same.

Another important point is that purpose creates meaning in your life, and meaning promotes health. Meaning can also give us the ability to overcome some serious odds, as in the case of Lance Armstrong. Many people view illness as a death sentence, while others view it as a challenge. Those who take it as a challenge and as part of their purpose are more likely to live long, prosperous lives. If you are suffering a life-threatening illness or an illness that has taken a lot out of you, try to think of the illness as a challenge and a purpose. Take from it what you can to help others who are facing such challenges. Research has shown that people who do just that may live longer.

Many people die when they believe their purpose is no longer needed. Victor Frankl, in Man's Search for Meaning, describes one example of this. Victor survived a German death camp in which most of the prisoners died. He could not figure out why so few people survived their time in the camp. He finally figured out that those who survived were those who still had purpose or a reason to live. They were those who took purpose from the experience, like Victor Frankl did. He took purpose from the experience and vowed that if he made it through the experience alive, he would make sure such horrors would never happen again. In his book he talks about the importance of meaning and purpose and how not having meaning and purpose can affect a person's health. In his situation having meaning and purpose was a major factor in survival and was the only way one could survive the camps. In short, without purpose, life will feel meaningless.

Most of us have heard about a relatively healthy person who spends years taking care of a sick spouse, and when the sick spouse dies, the surviving spouse dies soon after. The survivor's purpose was caring for the spouse, and when that purpose vanishes, the survivor gets sick himself, because he has lost his purpose in life. We sometimes see this in people who retire and sit around doing nothing but watching TV. From there they quickly age and end up sick, because their life has no meaning. The body recognizes when it is not being used for a meaningful purpose. In fact, a chemical change takes place, and age begins to show itself rapidly.

The body has a way of recognizing the lack of purpose and meaning in our lives. The way it does this is directly related to the way we feel. Our bodies respond to how we feel, so when we have no meaning, the body works less optimally. When we do have purpose, our bodies fight off disease with ease. How about when you have a very important event happening in your life? When I was in flight school, which lasts about three months, I never got sick, even when I was around people who were sick, like family members and friends. But as soon as training was over, I would get very ill and would be laid up in bed for a week or two. Completing training and not having a significant event to look forward to caused a lack of significance that weakened my immune system and led to illness. During the training, my body recognized the importance of the event and beefed up my immune system.

The point is this: when we are faced with meaningful tasks, our bodies protect themselves from illness and disease, but as soon as the body recognizes a reduction in stress, it lets its guard down and--WHAM--we get ill. It seems that happiness and fulfillment are the triggers to the positive chemicals our bodies produce--those that create health and prevent disease. This is one of the most important reasons we must have purpose in our lives. Our health depends on it, and so does our overall performance.

Another result of a lack of purpose and meaning is depression. Ask someone who is depressed what their purpose in life is, and they are very likely to respond, "I have no purpose, I am worthless." Most depression, I believe, is caused by a lack of purpose and meaning. As I said before, how we feel has a direct effect on our body's chemistry. I believe that most depression is caused by the effect of a long-term lack of purpose that literally changes the chemical structure of our bodies and leads to the depressed state.

What happens when a depressed person becomes well? They find a purpose, their life has new meaning, and they live a normal, happy life. Those who suffer from chronic depression often experience ups and downs where, for a period of time, their life has purpose, which gives their life meaning. The problem with chronic depression is that the person lacks a consistent sense of purpose and may be up one week and down the next, depending on what is meaningful to them at the moment. This is usually diagnosed as manic depression. Manic depressives may lack sufficient focus on what is important and end up being easily distracted. In other words, they tend to get bored easily with something and then go off without purpose and back into depression.

This cyclical lifestyle wreaks havoc on the person's chemical structure, and eventually those chemicals that make the person feel good become imbalanced. At this point, if purpose is found it will take significant time for the person's body to adjust its chemical structure so that it once again feels good. In other words, the person's body does not have time to provide the support necessary to feel good, so he or she ends up in a chronic state of depression. This is the point at which depression becomes difficult to cure.

The problem with trying to help people who suffer from depression is that it takes some time to readjust the chemical balance of the body before a consistent change is felt, and most do not feel like doing anything, let alone think of a purpose for their existence. If you can get someone thinking about their purpose long enough, they will find it. They will find true happiness and live a more fulfilling life. For some it takes more work then it does for others, but in the end the results will be the same. Find your purpose and your life will gain meaning. If you are one of these depressed people, the best medicine is to find your purpose and give your life meaning, and I promise your depression will vanish. It may be difficult to adjust your thinking in this regard, but with a big enough purpose anything is possible.

The Pillars of Excellence program will guide you in developing your own purpose and the ability to create meaning in your life. For now I want you to answer the following questions and keep them on hand--I suggest keeping a journal--until you complete this book. You may need them when you begin the practical section of the program, but at a minimum you will need to think about these questions when you begin to create your masterpiece, your life: What do you love about life? Think of everything you love about life and write it in your journal. What do you love to do? What are you good at? What would the perfect life look like for you? How can you give meaning to your life? This includes your job, family, friends, and all other areas of your life. From 1 to 10, with 10 being great and 1 being horrible, what level of purpose are you currently experiencing? Finally, what would your life have to be like for you to be fulfilled? Answer these questions honestly and do not rush.

Even if the tasks suggested here seem to be time-consuming, that time is brief compared to the rest of your life. You have your whole life ahead of you. The time to plan your life is now, not twenty years from now. When a person starts a business, they must first plan. This is no different for your own personal life. You need to get the plan on paper, and you need to know what you want your life to be about. Take the time now and do the required work that is needed to make your life a raving success, and you will not be sitting in your rocking chair twenty, thirty, or forty years from now saying, "I wish I would have . . . ." Now is the time to move, now is the time to act. You only have one chance on earth as far as we know, so make it worth something. Make it worth something to you, because in the end, you are the one you are going to be answering to, and you don't want to have to make excuses then. You will want to be proud of your life and of the accomplishments you have made. Remember, too, if you fail to plan now, you may not have twenty years left. If you do plan now, your life will have purpose, meaning, and fulfillment, and your chances of survival will increase tremendously.

Develop the motivation to survive, the drive to succeed, the spirit to shine, and the purpose to give meaning to your life. Get to know the true you, and move into true existence by knowing yourself and what you are all about. Love yourself and give yourself fully to life. Life needs you to perform and produce. That's really what we are here for, not to slump around sulking at the world because we feel we have been dealt a bad hand. For those of you who want to complain, remember: there are millions of people who have it worse off. But you can become the person you always knew you could be.

CHAPTER 4

THE PHYSICAL PILLAR

How would you like to wake up every morning at 6:00 a.m. with extraordinary energy and vitality? How about having the ability to fight off disease and reduce the chance of getting a cold, and even eliminating the possibility of developing life-threatening diseases? How would you like to add ten or even twenty quality years to your life? How about getting into the best shape of your life and reducing those unwanted pounds that have plagued you for the last few years? How would you like to be physically and mentally "in the zone" twenty-four hours a day? Wouldn't it be awesome to be more productive in one day than you used to be in one week? All this can be and will be yours when you follow the Pillars of Excellence program's guidelines for the Physical Pillar.

If we want to reach Optimum, it is imperative that our bodies are in good health. The Pillars of Excellence program promotes a balanced approach to living, and for this reason each pillar often requires more than one approach to affect it in positive ways. Our physical bodies are made up of different types of qualities that must be addressed if we are to get into optimum shape. The problem with most fitness programs is that they take a singular approach in that they focus on only one, or maybe two, types of exercises. Such an approach is better than nothing, but it is not Optimum. For optimum results we must aim for the best possible effect in all areas of our life by considering the five main areas that make up our physical being. These areas are anaerobic exercise, aerobic exercise, flexibility exercise, nutrition, and lifestyle.

Anaerobic exercise can be defined as exercise that does not require oxygen to perform and is best seen in strength sports such as weight lifting, gymnastics, and football. Aerobic exercise can be defined as exercise that requires oxygen to perform and is best seen in endurance sports such as running, biking, and swimming. Flexibility exercises are those exercises that extend rather than contract the muscle and are best seen in pre- or post-sport activities that get the muscle ready for high-intensity activity and thus reduce the possibility of injury. It is important to note that flexibility exercises can improve your strength if done properly. They can also help with endurance sports, because a muscle that is in flexible shape can hold greater amounts of ATP (adenosine triphosphate), which is the energy-producing chemical that provides the muscle with fuel and energy.

We all know about the nutrition ingredient of good physical health, but our world has been oversaturated with fad diets that can become quite confusing. The most important thing to remember for now is that your nutrition is the most important factor for your Physical Pillar and your health. Today we are faced with a plethora of diet and nutrition information that can get very confusing: one day a low-carb diet is best; the next day it's a high-carb diet. The Pillars of Excellence program will make nutrition much more understandable for you. You will see that healthy eating does not require a nutrition degree from Yale or having Mr. Olympia as a personal trainer. We will make it fun and very workable, and you will see and feel the results very quickly when you implement the suggestions for exercise and nutrition in the program.

I also want to make a point about exercise programs in general. Most personal trainers are overtraining their clients, and this leads to many problems, including the problem of reversing the desired effects of exercise. We live in a society that says more is better; for example, if someone says one pill is good, then ten must be better. We saw this in the carbohydrate craze of the 1980s, where we literally eliminated protein and good fats from our diet and consumed only carbohydrates. What happened next was a nation that had increased its fat by 12 percent, in some cases even more. Not only did our nation suffer the obesity, but also all the diseases, such as diabetes, that come along with being overweight and eating unhealthy amounts of certain foods.

People often get caught up in the newest fads and forget about the basics of good nutrition and proper exercise. My point is this: we must take all our actions with rationality and remember that balance is the most important aspect when it comes to proper exercise and nutrition. As for the overtraining, all I need to tell you is that the workouts recommended in the Pillars of Excellence program will be much more intense, but can be accomplished in about half the time of the typical exercise program. More is not always better; we must use our wisdom in all we do. To begin our discussion about creating wellness, I would like to discuss the trend of the health industry and how it affects not only your health, but also your pocketbook.

Today we live in a society that believes in medicine as the number one way to control disease. We have gotten to the point where we want to find a pill for every problem we have. The problem is that most medications have side effects, many of which require additional medication to combat the side effects from the initial medication. This can get so bad that one individual may be taking five to ten different prescriptions to treat one core disease. Why do we take so many pills? Why do we approach disease this way? Is there another approach? The answer to the last question is a huge YES! To answer it we must answer the first two questions.

Why do we take so many pills? The answer to this question may seem harsh, but it is true. We are lazy! The human brain can get very creative in finding ways to reduce workload and increase productivity. Infomercials flood the TV, telling us how their product can solve your problems. These commercials are trying to sell the easy way to do something. They are trying to sell you an easier way to live and solve your problems. This is especially true in the weight-loss industry. Ads on both TV and radio talk about miracle pills and supplements that can supposedly help you to lose weight. Some of these pills do work; they help you lose weight--at least temporarily--but this weight is often the wrong weight.

There are two ways to measure the weight of the human body. The number you see on your bathroom scale is an indication of your general weight. We also need to know composition, which can measure how much lean body mass we carry and how much body fat we carry. Lean body mass, or muscle, is tissue that requires energy to sustain it. Fat, on the other hand, does not need energy to sustain it. If we remove lean body mass, we also remove the body's ability to burn fat, because we lower the basic metabolic rate (BMR) when we lose muscle. When we do this, fat remains and the body becomes less efficient in losing fat. When we lose the right kind of weight--that is, fat--we do not affect the basic metabolic rate in a negative way. In fact, we often increase our BMR; therefore the body becomes even more efficient in losing fat.

Many of the fad diets and pills that promote weight loss do not consider the type of weight loss. They are merely selling the quickest way to lose weight, and that is by losing muscle. Muscle weighs more than fat, so losing weight by this method creates the illusion that you are losing a lot of weight. What most people don't understand, however, is that the weight is from loss of muscle tissue, which eventually causes the metabolism to slow, creating an increase in body fat resulting from the body's inability to burn what is taken in. This is why many people gain back the weight--and in most cases put back on more weight, fat weight--after a weight-loss diet that restricts the good food and consumes the bad. What happens is very complicated, but can be seen in our body's attempt at survival. When we restrict calories from the good source of food and eat more of the bad kind, the body believes it is actually starving. It then tries to compensate by storing as much food as possible for the famine ahead, storing the food as fat. To do this it slows the metabolism, which causes a reduction in energy. You begin to feel sluggish and tired. Your body is doing what it was designed to do, and that is to survive.

When we lose weight the healthy way, by losing fat, we see the opposite occur. Your body eliminates fat and keeps the muscle tissue--in some cases increasing muscle tissue--which increases your metabolism even more. In fact, your body weight may actually increase if you are eating right. The point is this: do not look at the scale to see how you are doing; instead, look at the loss of body fat. This can be done several ways. The first and easiest way is by noticing how your clothes fit. Keep in mind, though, that weight loss occurs from head to toe. In other words, you will begin losing weight from your head first, and then as you lose more and more fat, it will begin to come off the lower parts of your body. This means you may see a pear shape in the beginning, which can trick you into believing you are getting fatter, but you are not. Just be careful not to misinterpret your appearance, and remember how the body eliminates fat--it starts at the top and moves its way down.

There are more accurate ways to measure fat and lean body mass. One of these is to use fat calipers, which measure the thickness of a fold of skin with its underlying layer of fat. By doing this at key locations that are representative of the total amount of fat on the body, it is possible to estimate a person's total percentage of body fat. Another accurate but more expensive way to measure body fat is the hydrostatic method. Here you are weighed in a pool and your body composition is determined via buoyancy. Because fat is less dense than water, it floats. Thus, if your body is submerged in water, special equipment can be used to calculate your body composition to determine how much of it is lean and how much is fat. If you were ever lost at sea without a life preserver, having a greater percentage of fat would be a benefit. However, your chances of being lost at sea are significantly less than your chances of suffering from obesity-induced diseases.

Another accurate means of measuring body composition is called bio-electrical impedance. With this method electrodes are attached to different areas of your body. An electrical current is then sent through specific parts of your body that measures whether the current is being restricted or is free-flowing. It then uses that information to estimate the total composition of water in your body. Because muscle contains a greater percentaqe of water, the more water your body contains, the lower your body fat measurement will be. There is a minor problem with the test in that if you are dehydrated, the reading will be way off and will show a high body fat level. Thus, you must be hydrated when using this test to get accurate measurements.

All of these body composition measuring devices work--some are more expensive and some are more accurate--but all you need is to get an idea of your starting point and the direction you are going when you are losing body fat. For this reason, I would use the cheapest way, which is using the calipers. These tend to be less accurate, but they will give you the needed information so that you can adjust as necessary your diet and exercise programs to continue down the path of fat loss. It's best to use the same method consistently and have the same person perform the fat test, because your results will then be based on relative measurements. If you use different methods each time, you may not get the correct comparison. If you use a different person to help you measure every time, you will also run into the problem of not getting a consistent read, because each person does it a little differently.

When we consider pills for weight loss, we must remember the goal of the pill, which is to promote general weight loss--in other words, any kind of weight loss, whether it's muscle tissue, fat, or water. These pills don't look at just losing fat. In fact, the target weight loss would be from muscle, because that is the quickest way to lose weight. Most of the programs that use pills target muscle because of this fact. Many weight loss programs do nothing more than help you lose water weight in the beginning, and from there remove muscle weight, which creates a false reading of your true fat loss. The pills work by reducing your appetite and undernourishing your muscle tissue, which causes atrophy, the loss of muscle. Taking such "wonder pills" can also lead to malnutrition and a number of other health issues.

In addition to pills, a variety of powders and other formulas promise to help you lose weight with little or no effort on your part. I recently saw a commercial that claimed you could build muscle and exercise while you watched TV! Many of the dietary supplements that are advertised are not FDA approved, and many have never even been tested by the FDA. Many products claim to include a certain ingredient that is not actually present in the product. So we don't always know what we are taking, let alone whether it works or is safe. This can be dangerous and in some cases fatal. An example of this is a product called GHB (gamma-hydroxybutyric acid). Promoted as a dietary supplement with many benefits, and even sold in health food stores, GHB is actually a very dangerous chemical compound. In addition to being addictive, there have been many reports of death associated with GHB, which also has a reputation as a "date rape" drug.

The medical field is no better when it comes to trying to make us healthy. Today we are bombarded by commercials for prescription medications that scare the hell out of us by describing possible symptoms and then offering a fix by telling us to ask our doctor about their product. This is the typical pain-and-pleasure formula of drug advertising. The company describes the great pains you may be having and then offers you relief, or pleasure, from their product. In turn, when the doctor writes a prescription for a certain drug company's medication, the drug company pays the doctor. In other words, they are promoting the use of their drugs not with research alone, but with money as well by enticing doctors to promote and use the product. The companies reward doctors with money, trips to exotic places, dinners, and more.

Drug research is often skewed and many times tainted with untruths and hidden facts that in the end cause much damage to the consumer, the drug company, the doctor, and all involved. One recent example is the drug Vioxx, which was shown to cause problems, but its manufacturers ignored the research in favor of money and ignored the health of the consumer. Many of these drug companies know of problems with the drug and sell it anyway, hiding the truth from us and from our doctors, because they are more concerned about the investor and the bottom line than they are about the health of the consumer and the reputation of the doctor prescribing the drug.

In some cases, doctors prescribe even when a prescription is not needed. Why? To cover the loss of income resulting from the problems they experience with insurance companies; because the drug company provides doctors with incentives to prescribe their drug, they are tempted to prescribe more to increase their income. In fact, more than 70 percent of illnesses do not require a medication to correct, but look at how many times you have left the doctor's office without pills in hand--hardly ever! The loss of income doctors have experienced is no excuse for unethical behavior that can hurt their fellow man. Many of these charlatans should have their license pulled, and many of these drug companies need to be watched very closely.

There are many to blame for the problems in our health care, including consumers who go to the doctor at the first sign of a sniffle. Many parents often take their kids to the doctor--sometimes even the emergency room--for a cold or other non-threatening illness. Insurance companies are also to blame by taking control away from our health care professionals, dictating what they can and cannot do in terms of treatment, with money, not health care, being the number one consideration. Drug companies are not innocent either. When it comes to drug costs, perhaps it's true that they need to overcharge in order to recoup the costs of research, and it is this research that can benefit us in the long run, but that does not give drug companies the right to advertise by using scare tactics to encourage us to ask for a medication we don't even need. These drug manufacturers have made us a nation of pill poppers and drug addicts.

Look at what happened with antidepressants. For years we didn't know much about these drugs, but today many of them are household names, because drug companies aggressively promoted these drugs and made them so recognizable. We see ads for medications on the side of racecars, busses, and billboards--all over the place. These drugs have been prescribed irresponsibly, and many family physicians prescribe them at the first sign of feeling down. Life is a series of ups and downs. But we are taking people out of the game of life by numbing them to life and not allowing them to experience it the way it is supposed to be experienced. Don't get me wrong, some people need these drugs, but they need to be prescribed by someone who specializes in the area the medicine was made for, and they need to be prescribed with caution so that the user is getting the best possible option. Medical professionals are sworn to the Hippocratic oath, which says they will do no harm. But what the hell happened to this oath? It has only become a formality that means absolutely nothing.

Somewhere along the way the medical field got lost and went down the road of turning money into its number one priority and health its number two priority. This has to change, and the only way it can change is through us, as consumers. In order to do this we must know exactly what needs to change. To begin with, let us now consider what a doctor should do when it comes to his or her patients' health. As I said, doctors are in the business of making money, as are the insurance companies, since profit is the underlying goal. How do I know this? Look at it this way. If doctors are getting paid to prescribe certain medications, then it is safe to say that some of them will be motivated to prescribe those medications. If the doctor prescribes certain medications, they often have to prescribe another medicine to counteract side effects of the first medication they prescribed. This may go on several medications deep, and the patient ends up taking more medicine than was initially needed. In fact, many disease or medical problems come from the medical treatment of other diseases, and it has been shown that a large percentage of people end up as patients because of overly aggressive medical treatment.

On the insurance side, many insurance companies are public companies. The number one responsibility of the CEO of such companies is to make money for the stockholders, which they do, because if they don't, they could end up getting fired. They also tie a great deal of their salary and bonuses to profit, so profit becomes a motivating factor that often blinds them to reality. Since their number one job is to make money, why would they fund research for medicines that cure disease? They don't; instead they fund the research for drugs that cure symptoms, not diseases. They seem to believe that it is much more profitable to have a person take one pill a day of a certain medicine to cure his or her symptoms than it is to invest their money in developing a medication that will ultimately cure the disease. They also get the benefit of having to make more medication to cure symptoms that arise from the initial drug being prescribed. Sounds criminal, doesn't it? But it is, and it is happening every day.

How do we change this? Well, I first want to say that the change is going to be like kicking a battle ship, and it may seem that nothing can be done, but believe me when I say something can be done. The great news is that it will require nothing from you other than changing the way you look at treating disease. In fact, the benefit will be directly given to you, the consumer. The doctors and insurance companies will benefit as well, but they will be harder to convince, since they are making money with the current approach and the possibility of losing money scares the hell out of them. It is important to note that if the doctors and the insurance companies listen to this and implement it, they could benefit greatly and turn the industry around so that doctors could go back to making a great income and, more important, to promoting health as they were trained to do. The insurance companies are going to be the most difficult to motivate in this direction, but once they see the savings and increased profits, they too will jump on board. The bad news is they will probably continue down the road on which they are currently going and will lose out for quite some time. The good news is that you, the consumer, will attain benefit from day one, and then you will be the director of how you will be treated medically, not the other way around.

In order to be an informed consumer of the medical profession, we must first take a look at how we view disease. Disease is defined as a disorder or an abnormal condition of an organ or other part of an organism resulting from the effect of genetic or developmental errors, infection, nutritional deficiency, toxicity, or unfavorable environmental factors. So disease is really an abnormality, or a move from normal to abnormal, with regard to health. Whether this abnormality comes from genetic factors or from behavioral or environmental factors makes little difference in the view of insurance companies. Their concern should be for cure and the return to normal of the anomaly of the organism. For us and our doctors, on the other hand, whether the disease comes from genetic or behavioral or environmental is of significant importance. As consumers, we need to know if we can do something about it, and with most diseases something can be done by the consumer. As for the doctor, they too should be interested, because it is from this stand that they will decide the best route to take in treating the problem.

The next move is to look at disease from a different standpoint altogether. Ideally, for all diseases the focus should be on prevention. Why should we wait to get sick? Look at it this way. When we learn to drive, we are taught to drive defensively, which means we drive with the idea that we will prevent an accident. We are driving with prevention in mind. The same is true when it comes to car maintenance. We change the oil and perform general maintenance on the car for one purpose: to prevent problems, major problems, and keep the car running optimally. It makes me sick to think that the car industry has figured out that it is much more economical to prevent than it is to cure problems, while the medical industry is still in the archaic age trying to treat instead of prevent. Why can't the medical industry figure it out? Aren't they as intelligent as we have believed them to be? What this tells us is that either the medical industry's head is in the sand, or they are motivated by something other than medical ethics. I think it is the latter, but who knows and who cares as long as we, the consumer, understand what's going on.

Considering what we have learned, we can make some educated assumptions that make sense. First, it is much better to look at disease as something we want to avoid. It would be most beneficial for the consumer to prevent major illness if at all possible. Second, taking a preventive approach would be much healthier, and the consumer would benefit not only economically but in overall longevity and quality of life. The person would benefit in all areas of life and become an optimally functioning organism.

The next question is, how does this approach benefit insurance companies and doctors? To answer this we must look at the economics side of the equation, since we already understand that the motivating factor for insurance companies, drug companies, and doctors is money. With a focus on prevention, insurance companies would benefit mainly because of less disease and therefore fewer medical bills. This is because the prevention approach creates a healthier consumer, who will be less likely to end up with major health problems. Insurance premiums would then be lowered and the money directed to a coverage that promotes prevention. This could be done by reevaluating what insurance is for. Insurance is for problems we encounter that we can't afford to pay for on our own. Why is it that when we go to the doctor and are charged eighty dollars for a simple office visit, we don't pay it out of pocket, but instead charge it to the insurance company? We do it because we can. If the insurance companies got smart, they would figure out a way to stop this and get people paying for the doctor bills they can afford and leaving the ones they can't afford to the insurance company.

This could be done by offering the consumer a reduced rate and added benefits that promote prevention, such as gym memberships, health products, nutritional products, and the like. An insurance consumer could also get reduced rates for not including in their policies coverage for items they can afford and instead limiting their coverage for major problems they cannot afford. These consumers would be less likely to go to the doctor for general diseases for two reasons. The first is that if they are living in prevention, they are less likely to get sick. The second is that we often go to doctors when we don't need to, and with the prevention approach, consumers will be more careful in choosing when seeing a doctor is an absolute necessity.

How could the prevention approach positively affect the drug companies? Health and fitness products are projected to be one-tenth of our gross national product (GNP) in the next ten years. This is a staggering number; it indicates that the wellness industry is going to be a growing trend for new industries and a new career opportunity for people. This means there will be a huge market for health and wellness products and services. Nutritional supplements are increasingly becoming popular, and many of these supplements are being developed and produced by run-of-the-mill operations that need to be closed down anyway. Drug companies could get into this side of the business as well as the medicine side and make a killing. Think about it, one-tenth of our GNP, which is trillions of dollars just waiting to be made. This in itself is reason for the drug companies to endorse a prevention approach, and when they understand how much money can be made, they will endorse it. As a side benefit, if the drug companies get involved, they will rid the market of those fly-by-night operations that produce some pretty shady stuff, and we could clean this industry up once and for all.

How will the doctors benefit? There is an obvious answer, and again it is in the market of prevention. Doctors today specialize in disease and its cure. There will still be a need for this, since disease will always be a part of our environment. There will always be a few who do not follow the prevention approach, and those people will need the doctor who deals in disease. However, there will be a new field called prevention, and many doctors could revert to this very easily. They could now become health consultants, giving their patients information and prescriptions for healthier living. They could also become consultants to insurance companies in the development of prevention programs. Doctors could also get into personal training and nutritional areas, helping people develop personal wellness plans, including exercise and nutrition programs. They could also get involved in the corporate world, consulting with them on wellness for employees, which could lower rates for consumers and corporations for insurance. There are many more reasons for all fields to promote prevention, too many to cover here, but I think you get the picture.

All in all, everyone wins with the prevention approach, and we end up with good ethics to boot. Insurance companies will make their investments more profitable because the risk of disease is lowered, and in turn they can gain more consumers because of the lower premiums and affordability of insurance. The drug companies become big winners because they capitalize on the research and development of medicines that fight disease, prevent disease, and promote wellness. Doctors win because they become more ethical and motivated for the right reasons and make more money, since they too have a wider field of practice. Finally, consumers win in many ways. We win because we are rewarded for being healthy, and therefore we live healthier lifestyles, which create greater energy and productivity. We enjoy a life that is more fulfilling and higher in quality. We win because our insurance premiums go down and coverage goes up. This is because as it is now we often go to doctors when we don't need to, and if we live in prevention, we will be less likely to get sick. When we do get sick, we will be more receptive to allowing our bodies to correct the problems naturally. We win because we still get the major diseases covered by the insurance, as it was meant to be. Finally, we win because we will no longer be sold snake oil, invented drugs for invented diseases, medicine we don't need, and because we now have the benefit of having doctors who care for us for the right reasons. The whole economy wins because less money is spent on fixing preventable problems and more is spent on living well. All of mankind wins because we are making the survival of mankind more of a priority.

Let us now look at some preventive measures we can take to begin our health care in the right way. The Pillars of Excellence program focuses on health but also on fitness, because the two go hand in hand. It is a balanced approach. Most individuals who start an exercise program perform only one type of exercise. This is good--in fact, it is better than doing nothing--but an approach that provides us the ability to cover all bases of fitness is much more effective in that it focuses on the whole part of fitness. Look at it this way: returning to the car example, when we take care of our car and only focus on one major part of the car, we are not giving our car the ability to function optimally. The same is true for our fitness and health. If we focus on one part of fitness and health, we are not giving our bodies the opportunity to operate at Optimum.

As mentioned earlier, in the Pillars of Excellence program we focus on five main areas of health and fitness: anaerobic, aerobic, flexibility, nutrition, and lifestyle. Here we guide our clients in developing the most efficient program possible for the individual, realizing that there is much more to life than fitness. The program makes developing health and fitness simple and does not require you to become a recluse, where you have to spend all of your time fixing special meals and training to attain that optimum physical level. You will reach Optimum, and it will not require every minute of the day. We have done the research and development for you; all you have to do is take action.

Fitness should focus on realistic results and realistic effort to attain the goal you are trying to achieve. The philosophy of the Pillars of Excellence physical aspect is that of prevention and Optimum in terms of energy, vitality, longevity, and quality. We want you to have the aesthetic look you desire, but this is a symptom of our wellness and prevention program. In other words, your purpose of the Physical Pillar will be much more than just looking good. It entails the greatest benefit fitness and health has to offer, and that is a body that functions at its best, at Optimum. You will have the look of great health and fitness, and more important, you will develop the energy, vitality, longevity, and quality that we all need to live long, prosperous, and fulfilling lives.

The first thing we need to do in creating Optimum for your wellness is to define the characteristics of optimum health and fitness, or what the Pillars of Excellence calls wellness. Again, there are five general areas in the wellness arena: anaerobic, aerobic, flexibility, nutrition, and lifestyle. From these five aspects we developed an approach that is very effective in developing extraordinary health, fitness, and wellness. I know it sounds like a great deal of work, but I can assure you that the work required is very reasonable.

One point that I want to make is that for anyone to attain results and experience success, they must employ themselves in the process. In other words, this program is not going to be a cakewalk, and anyone who claims that their program is should be avoided at all costs. To attain anything of value requires work. This is important for two reasons. The first is that for anyone to achieve any goal, some work is required. The second reason is that a great deal of satisfaction in attaining any outcome is in the work itself. If you wanted to achieve an outcome, would you be as satisfied with the outcome if it were given to you, or would you be more satisfied if you had to work to attain the outcome? The answer to this is sometimes not very obvious, but the truth is that any outcome that requires our effort is the one that provides the greatest reward. In fact, it is the work that fulfills us, not the outcome.

The goal is the carrot that gives us the ability to look forward to the final goal, which gives us purpose, but it is not the true reward.

For example, when we are waiting for an event that we are looking forward to, like a goal or a vacation, we often realize that the anticipation leading up to the event is much more fun then the event or goal itself. Take, for instance, the Monday blues and the Friday joys. On Monday many people often feel depressed or unmotivated, but on Friday they feel happy and motivated. Why? Monday they can't see anything that reflects enjoyment in the immediate future, but Friday they see the weekend and not having to face the same old job. They are looking forward to doing something they enjoy doing, whatever that may be. In fact, we can attribute depression to not having anything to look forward to. For those who are depressed, life has no meaning because there is nothing to anticipate. Those who are happy and fulfilled are that way in part because they have something to look forward to. The point is this: working to attain something is often the part of the process we do not recognize as the part that brings the greatest happiness and fulfillment. The work toward a desirable goal is what creates the happiness and fulfillment; the goal itself is merely a motivating factor. The work and the goal together provide us with the purpose and meaning we seek to make life exciting and enjoyable. Appreciate the work, and you will find yourself actually looking forward to the work and therefore attaining a much sweeter outcome.

Optimum wellness, in short, supports your ability to function at your true physical potential. This means that you have the energy to withstand your daily activities, the vitality to enjoy physical activity with others, longevity to enjoy life on earth as long as possible, to enjoy your offspring's success and the success of your grandchildren, and a quality of life that gives you the freedom to care for yourself and produce positive outcomes in all areas of your life. Optimum wellness allows you to enjoy life without constant illness; therefore, optimum wellness takes a preventive stand in relation to medical care. In other words, optimum wellness sees preventing disease, not curing it, as the first line of defense. With this in mind, the first action you can take toward optimum wellness is in choice. Here you choose the lifestyle that focuses on prevention and can be seen in decisions that affect your ability to prevent disease. For example, if you smoke, you may choose to quit smoking, since this is the number one cause of cancer and has negative effects on our heart and other organs as well. Another example is if a person decides to reduce stress by choosing not to get angry or to get help in controlling their anger. The point is that our choices are the first and most powerful action we can take to make a difference in our wellness.

The next area we will cover in detail is exercise. Three of the five main areas of health are related to exercise: anaerobic, aerobic, and flexibility. It is important to discuss how each of these areas affects our wellness to understand their importance with regard to our health.

We will begin with anaerobic. As mentioned above, our anaerobic fitness is the fitness that produces strength. This includes muscle strength, bone strength, and tendon strength. There is also a residual affect on other areas of our fitness as well, like our heart, lungs, and other organs, but for the sake of keeping things simple, we will only discuss the major effects each area of fitness has on our wellness.

Anaerobic work is defined as work without oxygen. In other words, anaerobic exercise does not require a great amount of oxygen to perform. For the purpose of energy, our anaerobic strength is directly related to our muscle hypertrophy, or growth. When we provide more living tissue, as we do when we add muscle and bone density, our body's metabolism speeds up, and in turn our energy goes up. The nice thing about this is that since our metabolism increases, so does our ability to burn fat.

It should be noted that anaerobic exercise is much more effective in depleting fat cells than aerobic exercise over the long run. This may sound surprising, because many people believe that aerobic exercise creates the greatest fat burn. However, over time anaerobic exercise causes your metabolism to increase more than aerobic exercise because of the added living tissue that anaerobic exercise provides with muscle hypertrophy. It may be true that fat loss is more prevalent during aerobic exercise than it is during anaerobic exercise, but in the end anaerobic work leads to the greatest amount of fat loss because of the gain in living tissue. Aerobic exercise does not allow for muscle hypertrophy or gain, and therefore your metabolism is only affected during the work itself. In fact, too much aerobic activity can actually hinder the body's ability to burn fat, since it is geared to survive. If one ends up in a state of simulated starvation, the metabolism will slow.

With regard to vitality, our anaerobic factor provides us with the ability to maintain higher levels of survival capacity, because it gives us the power to live vigorously. We are able to perform physical activities more optimally because of the greater muscle, bone, and tendon strength.

As we age we begin to waste in that we lose muscle mass and strength, which causes a loss of energy, vitality, quality, and possibly longevity. When we perform anaerobic activity we reduce this wasting, and in some cases we can even reverse it in the beginning, therefore slowing the aging process. Reversing the aging process allows us to experience life with more energy, vitality, and tenacity. We are then able to live more physically active lifestyles that provide us with the ability to enjoy life more fully.

When looking at the quality factor of life, there is a direct correlation between strength and quality, because we are more able to do things when we are fit within the anaerobic realm. When we improve our anaerobic fitness, we in turn enjoy life more fully. This relates to more living as we age and therefore greater fulfillment. We are not dealing with having to sit on the sidelines of life and watch others enjoy life's activities. Anaerobic fitness also reduces the possibility that our loved ones will be burdened with caring for us when wasting gets the best of us. Having greater anaerobic fitness gives us greater independence, therefore freedom to enjoy life. We also must consider the burden we put on our families. When we don't take care of ourselves, we are disrespecting those around us, because someday they may have to take care of us. If we can put that off as long as possible, or even prevent it altogether, we are respecting others tremendously. Think about how selfish it is to act in ways that hurt you, because in the long run it will be hurting others as well.

Now let's look at the longevity factor. How long we live is not as important as how well we live. As mentioned above, anaerobic fitness allows us to live with greater function ability, therefore greater quality. As for longevity, we may be able to extend our lives with greater anaerobic fitness, but even if it only gives us a year or two, we are living more years of our life in quality, which in general gives us more opportunity to produce and live more fulfilling lives. In short, even if we do not add any years to our life, we automatically gain greater living from greater productivity. Would you want to live to the age of eighty spending the last ten years of life dependent on loved ones or professionals caring for you? Or would you rather live to eighty depending on yourself and producing till the day you die? I would assume that most would want to live the last years of their lives living productively. Everyone is different, but I think you get the idea.

Now let's look at the aerobic factor of health, fitness, and wellness. Aerobic fitness pertains to endurance and can be defined as exercise that requires oxygen to perform. Unlike anaerobic exercise, aerobic exercise involves greater oxygen consumption and raises your heart rate for an extended period of time. In short, aerobic exercise is low in intensity and long in duration, while anaerobic exercise is short in duration and high in intensity. The benefits that are experienced with aerobic exercise are plentiful, and in the area of energy, aerobic exercise awards you the benefit of greater efficiency in blood movement and even volume. When you are in good aerobic shape, your heart and lungs are more efficient and are able to handle more physical and mental activity. In other words, your heart has the ability to pump more blood with each stroke; therefore, it does not have to beat as fast or as hard to perform the work needed. Also, your lungs are more capable when you are fit aerobically, so your breathing allows for greater efficiency; therefore, more oxygen is replenished and sent to the body with greater efficiency. All of this gives your body the ability to operate with less energy expenditure, leaving you with greater energy to burn.

In the area of vitality, an aerobically fit body allows you to endure longer periods of work, play, and greater opportunity of productivity. Of course when we produce, we are more fulfilled and we then live happier lives, which aerobic fitness promotes.

Looking at quality, we can see that aerobic exercise gives us greater efficiency and greater endurance, which gives us the ability to work, play, or be more active for longer periods of time. The more active one is, the happier and more fulfilled they will be.

When you exercise aerobically you also clean out your lymph system. In general your lymph system is somewhat like your blood system, but it does not have the pump, so a great deal of the fluid sits stagnant and does not move very much. When you exercise aerobically, it acts like a pump to your lymph system and moves the fluid through more rapidly, causing greater effects of immune and other important functions with relation to prevention of disease. Another great way to affect the lymph system is to perform power breaths, which also helps the lymph fluid move. To do power breaths all you need to do is inhale for a count of 1, hold for a count of 4 and exhale for a count of 2. In other words, a ratio of 1:4:2. For example, you could inhale for a count of 7, hold for a count of 28 and exhale for a count of 14. Power breaths will also wake you up, so you can do them first thing in the morning for a good wake-up exercise.

As for longevity, one can see many benefits of aerobic fitness. When we perform aerobic exercise, we strengthen our heart, lungs, and lymph system, so we experience greater cardiovascular fitness, which helps prevent heart disease and cancer, to name just two benefits. There are many more positive effects, but this in itself gives you enough reason why it is beneficial to maintain aerobic fitness.

Let's discuss flexibility, which involves muscle suppleness. Flexibility is of great importance for our ability to live with energy, vitality, longevity, and quality. Being flexible gives us greater mobility, improved strength, and greater muscle endurance because of its capability to increase cell size and ATP storage and prevent injury. With regard to energy, our muscles need a chemical called ATP to generate activity potential. With regard to vitality, the more we can move, the more we can perform survival activities like exercise and work. When we can perform activities, we are given greater abilities to live and in turn get more out of life. Your quality of life is also improved with greater flexibility, because you are able to do more. When we age our muscles become less supple or stiffer, limiting our ability to perform. This generally limits our life, which reduces quality of life. We also see an increase in longevity because of the body's response to all forms of exercise, in that it positively enhances the body's chemical environment and gives many wellness benefits.

With all forms of exercise we see another great benefit in the area of chemical response. When we exercise, whether it is anaerobic, aerobic, or stretching, we create the body's need and ability to create positive chemicals like GH and endorphins. GH is growth hormone, a chemical that is tied to youth. It is the hormone that gives us our ability to create other hormones, such as testosterone and estrogen. Many of these chemicals allow us to regenerate muscle tissue and regenerate our youthful appearance. Thus, these are the chemicals that keep us looking and feeling young and, to a degree, help us stay young.

All forms of exercise promote endorphins, and it should be mentioned that these endorphins create a sense of well-being. We all have experienced what is called a "runner's high," or at least most of you have heard of this term. It is very real and is similar to the high one experiences when taking heroin. In fact, endorphins can be very addictive, which is the reason many people get to the point where exercise is a must for them in order to feel good. In other words, they look forward to the exercise, because they know how they are going to feel when they are finished. The exercise is their fix, and their body craves this fix. Now, some people will say that a lot of exercise is unhealthy, but our bodies do things for a reason, and in order to survive, we have been given this ability to produce endorphins in part so that we will seek movement in the form of exercise to give us the benefit of fitness. There are, however, some people who do take it to extremes, so before we move on to nutrition I want to talk about how much exercise people need.

What is a reasonable amount of exercise? To answer this we must consider our purpose. Some people exercise to improve athletic abilities, while others perform exercise for general wellness. When it comes to exercising in order to enhance our energy, vitality, longevity, quality and preventive abilities, anything that takes us out of this can be considered other than that which promotes wellness. In other words, if a person is running twenty miles a day, we can safely say that the benefits eventually start to wane and even begin to deteriorate to the point of having negative effects. No one can cell precisely where these negative effects occur, but we are capable of reading our bodies in order to find that perfect amount of exercise.

Your body will tell you very specifically if what you are doing to it is harmful or helpful. For example, we sometimes feel pain when we exercise. Now, please understand that there are different kinds of pain, and there is a distinct difference between the pain we experience with positive exercise and the pain we experience from doing too much exercise. The pain one feels when they exercise is a burning sensation from the lactic acid that develops during exercise. The pain we feel from injury is quite different in that it is sharper. In short, you will know the difference if you listen to your body. Those who perform too much exercise, to the point of injury, have problems controlling their psychological factors and also have problems elsewhere, like in their self-esteem. I am not saying that people who run marathons have low self-esteem. I am saying that anyone who exercises to the point of injury is suffering from some psychological anomaly that needs to be addressed. Just be careful and let your body be the judge.

The next physical factor with regard to wellness is that of nutrition. Nutrition is probably the most effective aspect with regard to any one of the wellness factors. All of the fitness factors together give the greatest benefit, so don't ignore everything but nutrition. But nutrition is a very key point in all wellness activities, and without it you are fighting a losing battle.

Nutrition has been a very confusing factor, because everyone wants to know the quickest and easiest way to lose weight. This has led to many problems, because many people have developed certain diets based on weight loss alone and not overall health. There are literally thousands of diets out there, and it is difficult to figure out which one is the best. To find the best diet for you, you must answer the following question: How do I eat to provide my body with the optimum amount of proper nutrition that will feed my body for the greatest survival potential? This means that you must develop a diet that will give you the greatest amount of energy, vitality, quality, and longevity. The Pillars of Excellence program has developed such a nutrition plan, and you are about to learn about the diet your body was designed to eat. It is not some fad diet that will require ridiculous eating habits, and you are not going to have to plug your nose to get the food down your throat. You will be able to enjoy it, get amazing results fairly quickly, and, most important, you will feel better then you have ever felt before.

To begin, I think it is best to start with the Pillars of Excellence nutrition philosophy. Many people eat for the taste; they enjoy food as a pleasure instead of looking at food as a health factor. Like everything we put into our bodies, whatever it is will have an effect on our bodies, and this is no different with food. In fact, all substances have either a positive effect or a negative effect. This holds true for drugs as well, and food should be used like a drug, with care and caution. It is must be used for the betterment of that wonderful gift you have been given, your body. The first thing I want you to understand is this: when you eat, you should eat for nutrition, not for taste. This does not mean you have to eat foods you do not like; I just mean that you should look at food as nutrition for your body and not as some pleasure treat.

Anyone who questions the importance of eating the right foods, just remember this. Would you put oil in your car if the oil were contaminated? NO! Would you put anything in your car if you knew it would harm it? NO! So why would you put food into your body that is contaminated or that would harm it in any way? When I say "contaminated," I mean anything that will not allow your body to perform optimally. When you view food as a drug, you will treat it much more differently and use it as it was intended to be used--as a drug to heal and rejuvenate your spirit, body, and mind.

It is best to break nutrition into two areas: micronutrients and macronutrients. Micronutrients are vitamins and minerals, while macronutrients are proteins, carbohydrates, and fats. For the sake of simplicity, it is important to understand micronutrients, but all one needs to know is that micronutrients are vitamins and minerals that allow your body to heal at the cellular level. I'm not a big believer in taking mass quantities of any type of supplement. However, I am a believer in trying to take in the optimum amount of substances in order to support your body's ability to function at its best, and this holds true for micronutrients as well.

Micronutrients today are very important, especially with our poisoned and polluted environment. They also allow us to deal with the stress of everyday living. Much of our food is actually lacking in micronutrients, which causes malnutrition and a number of health problems. Many of our youth today are actually malnourished. I know this is hard to believe, especially since obesity seems to be a great problem. But it is possible to be overweight and malnourished if the food we ingest contains empty calories and an overabundance of sugar.

It is imperative that we get the adequate amount of vitamins and minerals to support our body's functions. Today much of the food we eat, even vegetables and fruits, lack the proper amount of micronutrients because of the overuse of soil and other factors.

For this reason, I believe it is important to supplement your diet with a multiple vitamin and mineral supplement. I don't believe in oversupplying your body with anything, and this includes vitamins and minerals, but I do believe that we should get the proper amount of micronutrients, and one way to do this is through supplementation.

The correct amount of micronutrients can be obtained by eating a well-balanced diet and taking a multiple vitamin and mineral supplement at least every other day. It is also important to drink plenty of water; but again, I do not believe in too much of anything, and this includes water. You don't have to drink a gallon of water every day in order to get adequate amounts, but you need to get at least sixty ounces a day. If you drink a large glass of water with every meal, you will be ingesting enough water for optimum performance. In order to get enough micronutrients, it is imperative for you to eat a well-balanced diet and take a multiple vitamin and mineral supplement daily, drink plenty of water, and try to get as much of your food in its natural form as you possibly can.

Macronutrients are proteins, carbohydrates, and fats. It is important to get the proper macronutrient portions in order to get the most efficient benefit from the food we ingest. Our bodies can only assimilate a certain amount of any substance, including food, at any given time. Our bodies are capable of digesting a certain amount of protein, carbohydrates, and fats in a given amount of time. If we eat too much of any of the macronutrients, our bodies will store it as fat and eliminate the rest.

Our bodies are survival organisms, and the amount the body holds as fat depends not only on the amount of nutrition it is getting, but also on the feeding schedule. The less good nutrition we get, the more fat our bodies store, and the closer we get to the optimum amount of good nutrition, the more food will be used and the remaining eliminated. Because we are generally undernourished and overfed, we tend to hold on to more fat than is required. To eat properly will take some practice, but once you get the hang of it, you will not notice any difference from how you eat now.

When you receive a prescription from your doctor, you are given specific instructions on how to take the medicine, where the medicine is often given several times a day. This is done because your body can only digest a specific amount of any substance in a given amount of time. Food is no different, as your body is unable to digest any food beyond a given amount. This depends on several factors, including your activity level and your body's metabolism. For this reason it is very important to understand how often you should eat and how much you should eat. It is also important to understand the ratio of proteins, carbohydrates, and fats that you should eat in any given meal. I know this is starting to sound a bit complicated, but I can assure you that the Pillars of Excellence program has developed a way to make it simple. I am only giving you this information so you can understand how food works and how your body deals with food, because the more you know, the better you will get.

Your body is a survival machine, and it does certain things under certain circumstances. Your body is very effective in dealing with both a lack of nutrition and an abundance of nutrition. It functions with one thing in mind, and that is survival. If you do not eat enough, your body will eventually begin a process of protecting you from malnutrition.

When a person goes on a restricted diet, their body goes through specific changes, and if the calories are too low, the body will go into a state of metabolic momentum. Approximately four days after a person begins to restrict calories, he or she experiences a great increase in energy and are not able to sleep. This is the body's way of giving you the energy needed to go hunt for food so that you can start to feed its needs. The problem arrives when the food is restricted after a period of time, where the body then starts to slow its metabolism so that it can conserve what it has left. This creates a great loss of energy, and you may feel tired and irritable. Eventually your body shuts off the hunger mechanism, and you no longer feel the hunger pains. You begin to lose muscle mass, which depletes your metabolism even further, and anything you eat at this point gets stored as fat.

If a person eats too much food after going on a restricted diet, the body then prepares for the next famine by taking all the food that is ingested and storing it as fat. This is why many people who go on calorie-restricted diets gain more weight than when they began eating as they did before the initial diet. The body's metabolism does not speed up, because most of the food is being put into fat cells and not developing muscle cells. Muscle cells are living tissues; therefore, they require energy to live. On the other hand, fat cells require no energy to live, since they are not living tissue; your metabolism slows and you end up gaining fat. This begins a crazy cycle of developing greater amounts of fat over a given period of time.

How much food should one eat? Many nutritionists actually have their clients weigh their food and invoke very strict rules about the perfect amount. Such a practice is time-consuming and is one key reason that many people don't complete the weight-loss process. A very effective way to measure your food is to understand that a serving is about the size of your palm. For example, if you are going to have a meal, you can measure the amount of each macronutrient, except the fats, in the palm of your hand, and whatever fits in your palm is the serving size of that macronutrient. We will discuss this further in just a little bit.

Portion size is only one part of the equation, and we must also pay attention to the type of macronutrients we eat. Proteins come in different forms and can be broken down into two types: complete proteins and incomplete proteins. Proteins that have the proper amount of amino acids are complete proteins; those that do not have the proper amount of amino acids are incomplete proteins. Our job is to try to ingest complete proteins, because our bodies need the complete protein sources in order for protein to do its job. Proteins have a rating system, which is directly connected to the number of amino acids each protein contains. If the proteins in a food lack a sufficient profile of amino acids, that food's rating is lower, while proteins that contain sufficient amounts of amino acids rate higher on the scale. Egg whites are a good example of a protein that is complete, and the body can use it most efficiently.

On the other side are vegetable proteins, which are not as effective, since the protein is incomplete. Vegetable proteins are incomplete proteins because they lack the proper amino acid ratio. It is very difficult for a vegetarian to get the proper amount of protein in their diet, since their diet consists of incomplete proteins. This is not to say that vegetarians can't get the adequate amount of protein needed, but it is extremely difficult to do so, since it requires a great deal of effort in combining certain vegetables and certain other foods to develop a complete protein. In fact, it is next to impossible to do it on a regular basis and can be very time-consuming.

In general, you should have five to six servings a day of high-quality protein from lean meats, egg whites, and other quality sources. This will give your body adequate amino acids to repair the damage to your cells. It will also be enough to develop the muscle tissue required to effectively handle the workload you face.

Carbohydrates are an extremely important nutrient when it comes to fat development, fat reduction, and overall general health and wellness. There are two types of carbohydrates: high glycemic index carbohydrates and low glycemic index carbohydrates. High glycemic index carbohydrates are those that contain high levels of sugar in the form of simple sugar or carbohydrates that act as simple sugars. They enter the bloodstream quickly. Low glycemic index carbohydrates contain low levels of simple sugars and are generally considered complex carbohydrates. They enter the bloodstream at a slower pace. The important point is the level of sugar the carbohydrate contains, because this will dictate the way it will be assimilated and the amount and speed at which insulin is disseminated throughout the body.

Once the carbohydrates have been ingested, the body will produce insulin. The amount of insulin and the speed at which it is released into the body are dependent on the glycemic index of the carbohydrate. For example, table sugar is a high glycemic index carbohydrate, and the body will release rapidly a large amount of insulin to combat the high blood sugar. If your insulin is doing its job, it will eliminate the blood sugar fairly quickly and bring your blood sugar down below normal. This low blood sugar then triggers hunger, even though your body does not need the food. The hunger it triggers is also in the form of sugar cravings, because your body registers low blood sugar. This hunger leads you to seek out sweets and consume sugar again, therefore starting a vicious cycle, which is the reason we see so much obesity today.

Another problem occurs in this cycle. When your body dispenses a large quantity of insulin to fight off large quantities of sugar, you will eventually have no sugar in your blood and only free-roaming insulin. This free-roaming insulin tells the cells of your body to hold on to any nutrition that comes in and store it as fat. It does this because the body is surviving and it recognizes the low blood sugar as a famine, so it prepares for the famine by triggering the body to store nutrition as fat. It also slows the metabolism, which in turn causes us to burn less energy, so we feel tired and lethargic and end up sleeping or just sitting around.

Not only do you get the vicious cycle of low blood sugar and high blood sugar that creates sugar cravings, but you also get the added problem of sensitive fat cells wanting to suck up more nutrition and increase in size and number. In short, you become fatter, and eventually you reach the diagnosis of obesity. This is a horrible cycle, and it creates many of the health problems we see today.

With regard to carbohydrate portion, again we make this as simple as possible. Try to eat low glycemic index carbohydrates with your protein in the amounts that fit in the palm of your hand. Since you are eating the carbohydrates with your protein, you'll be ingesting five to six servings a day. Remember, a serving size is the amount that fits in the palm of your hand.

There are two types of fats: saturated fats and unsaturated fats. Saturated fats are those that solidify at room temperature and are usually the cause of high cholesterol and blocked arteries. Unsaturated fats are those that stay liquid at room temperature. Monounsaturated fats are an example of a fat that remains liquid at room temperature, and they are the ones we want to ingest. I want to make sure you understand that it is almost impossible to remove all bad fats from your diet, and for this reason some of the fat you will consume will be saturated fat. This is okay as long as you limit saturated fats as much as possible.

The monounsaturated fats are the fats that are heart-healthy fats, which give us the ability to prevent and fight off heart disease as long as we don't over-ingest them. The serving size of fats is different than proteins and carbohydrates. Fats carry higher calories per gram; therefore, it is important to understand that most of your fat intake can be gained from your protein source. However, it is imperative that you get enough monounsaturated fats, and for this reason you should supplement your diet every day with two to three teaspoons of flaxseed oil with two to three of your meals.

In appendix 2 I have provided you with a simple way to make sure you are getting the proper foods in the proper proportions. You will notice that there are four columns: one for protein, one for carbohydrates, one for vegetables, and one for fats. With regard to vegetables, all you need to know is that you should try to consume a variety of them, making sure to obtain the major portions from green leafy types of vegetables. In general, this chart is very easy to use; all you have to do is pick one food source from each column at each meal in the size that fits in the palm of your hand, except for the fat column. This column has specific instructions to follow. This will assure that you get the proper amount and the proper ratio of proteins, carbohydrates, and fats. There are several different choices for each category, so you should not have a problem finding the foods you will enjoy.

I want to make certain you understand the number of meals that should be eaten each day. In the beginning you may not be used to eating so frequently, since many of us are used to consuming only two or three meals a day. However, it is important that you get four to six meals a day; shoot for four meals the first few days, and then gradually increase the number of meals you have in a day within the first two weeks. At this point, you should consume six meals a day spread out every three to three and one-half hours.

It is imperative to eat six meals a day, since your body will recognize this state as having plenty of nutrition, which will then allow fat to be removed. In short, when you consume enough nutrition, spread out evenly throughout the day, your body will no longer need the extra fat for the famine it thought it was experiencing when it was only receiving two or three meals a day. I know it sounds a bit off the wall, but trust me. In the beginning, you may feel as though you are gaining weight. You may even gain a pound or two within the first few weeks, but once your metabolism kicks in, your body will burn the fat off fairly rapidly.

It's important to understand that your body will require some time to adjust, so gaining weight in the beginning is almost a necessity. In order for your metabolism to kick in, your body will have to feel comfortable knowing the famine no longer exists. If you want to see something interesting, follow this procedure: begin taking your temperature first thing in the morning on Day 1 of your new diet. This should be done immediately when you wake, so place a thermometer next to your bed and take your temperature before you get out of bed. After a couple of weeks, your temperature will actually increase by a degree when your metabolism kicks in. This will be the indication that your metabolism is beginning to burn at a higher rate, and from here you will begin losing body fat. You will also notice an increase in energy, which will be consistent throughout the day.

There are many factors that can lead us to eat unhealthily, and one of these factors is stress. Stress is the number one killer; in other words, it is the number one reason people get disease. It causes heart problems, cancer, and other problems, because it lowers the immune system. When we are stressed, we have a tendency to go to food or other behaviors that take our mind off of the stressful situation. We often eat to change our emotional state, which causes a host of problems. One of the best ways to control stress is to begin eating properly, getting plenty of rest and drinking plenty of water. At first it may be difficult to change your approach and not choose the negative behaviors to mask the stress, but once you feel the effects that a good diet and plenty of rest offer, you will soon seek out the pleasure that doing so provides. I can't stress this enough: having the ability to control the behavior that causes one to overeat the wrong foods is of critical importance.

You should never feel hungry on this diet; if you do, you are not getting enough nutrition. If this happens, you need to increase your food intake by a half a meal. In other words, if you are eating five meals a day and hunger sets in, then add half a meal, or half servings, so that now you are taking in five and one-half meals. Remain at this meal intake for two days, and if you are still hungry, add another half a meal so that you will be eating six full meals. Do this until you are not hungry. It is important to be satisfied if you want to lose body fat. If you are not satisfied, you will be more likely to revert to your old eating behaviors. Eating healthy should be pleasurable, and the Pillars of Excellence nutrition program will allow this. It was designed to meet the needs of your body and reduce the psychological effects of stress and other problems associated with changing eating habits.

Another way to reduce stress is to simply take a few deep breaths and get into the moment so that you recognize your desires as a symptom of stress rather than as true hunger. Reduce your stress as much as you possibly can, because stress can also cause you to gain body fat as well. When you are stressed out, your body produces a chemical called cortisone, which causes your body to eat muscle cells and in turn reduces muscle weight. This slows your metabolism, and you begin to add fat because of the reduced energy consumption. This also makes you feel tired and lethargic so that activity is out of the question, and again there is another reduction in energy burned.

Lifestyle is an extreme factor when it comes to becoming physically and psychologically healthy. Your choices are of extreme importance to your physical health, and you should learn to live a life that is wellness-based, where you work to prevent disease instead of waiting for the disease to hit and then dealing with it. The Pillars of Excellence program believes in preventive maintenance, where preventing disease is actually much more efficient then dealing with disease.

Developing an exercise program can get extremely complicated while you are developing a nutritional program. If this becomes too complicated for you, I suggest hiring a personal trainer and a nutritionist to guide you in the process. We do offer individual coaching in which we will help you develop an exercise program and nutrition program based solely on your individual needs, but it is important for you to have someone to guide you in using exercise equipment and food preparation. Remember, any endeavor requires the development of knowledge on your part if you are to perform it at optimum levels, so find yourself some good sources of information and learn as much as you can about your body, then use that information to improve all aspects of your health.

CHAPTER 5

THE MENTAL PILLAR

The Mental Pillar separates us from the animal kingdom. It separates us from the third world and allows us to function on a higher plain. What we can do mentally is still unknown, but it is safe to say that we have only scratched the surface and much more potential is expected to be discovered. Here we will teach you how the brain works, give you the ability to operate it at optimum levels, and give you the ability to use your mind to generate knowledge, wisdom, skill and creativity.

To begin I would like to define knowledge. Many say that knowledge is power, which is partly true. But knowledge is only potential power if it is never used; therefore, for knowledge to become powerful it must be used in some way, shape, or form to increase your ability to maintain the survival dynamics in a way that improves the quality of your life and the lives of those around you. It is important to understand that knowledge is not just remembering facts. It is much more than remembering; it is the ability to put to use what you learn for the benefit of greater survival opportunity.

Our education system is set up to teach knowledge from a theoretical standpoint. In other words, the student is tested on data and not his or her ability to use the data. It is a known fact that many college graduates leave college with the ability to recite, from memory, knowledge that they could never use. It takes experience on top of this knowledge for them to put it to use effectively. For example, you would not give an architect coming out of college the job of building the tallest building in the world. Why is this? Because the student was taught to memorize data only; he or she was not given any practical learning in the area of architecture. Sure, they put together some models and other types of practical exercises that related to architecture, but they never built an actual structure.

A student leaving college should be able to complete any task in the area of their interest. In other words, the student should have the knowledge, wisdom, skill, creativity, and ability to perform in his or her area of expertise. The sad truth is they cannot, and society is suffering because of it. So this brings me to our first rule when it comes to developing our minds. We should look at all learning in terms of how we can apply it to our life and if it will work. In short, when we complete the study of any subject, we should be able to use it on a practical level in realistic environments.

Learning is a very complicated task, because we have never really been taught to learn. What is the most effective way to learn? This is a question that has never been completely answered, but it is imperative that we understand how to learn and what we should expect when we truly learn anything. For now let's just say that learning a topic should entail a person's ability to use his or her knowledge in reality in order to successfully implement the knowledge gained, and to use that knowledge to fully and completely understand all concepts. To do this requires a specific set of actions one must follow in order to truly understand any topic.

Your first step in learning any new topic should be to understand the vocabulary of that subject. We often read and pass words we don't really understand and continue reading, thinking we can figure it out as we go. But this usually doesn't work well, and for effective learning to take place, it is imperative that you understand every word that you read on a given page. We have all experienced situations where we are reading and eventually realize that we didn't understand a thing on the page. This may be because somewhere in our reading we passed a word we didn't understand. If we are to truly comprehend the topic, we must go back and find the word we didn't understand, look it up in a dictionary, and learn it so that we can move on and understand what we are reading. This may take some time in the beginning, but it is essential to understand the vocabulary of that topic if we want to learn the topic fully.

In the study of any topic it is important to begin a text by circling or writing down all the words that you do not understand. Look the words up in the dictionary and learn not only their definition, but get familiar with the word, understanding its origin, its other meanings, and any other information you can find on that particular word. It is important that you truly understand the meaning of the word, since words often have several different meanings. To fully understand the word, you must go through the definition and understand the appropriate meaning for the appropriate situation and then apply that word to several different sentences to assure yourself you understand what it means. Once you understand the meaning of that word, then move on to the next word, and do this until you complete all words on that page. Once you understand all the words on that page, go back and read the page, and never go past the point of not understanding. If you find a another word that you do not fully understand, do the same thing until all words on the page are fully understood.

Another important factor in learning is the concept of gradient. Gradient is the rate at which something is experienced. In learning this can be demonstrated in the example of a child learning to ride a bike. If the child is using training wheels and you are going to teach him to ride without training wheels, you would not want to pull the training wheels off, put the child on the bike, and expect him to ride it. In this example, the gradient is too steep. If you take the training wheels off and hold the bike without letting go, he would never learn to ride it, because eventually he will get tired of you running behind him. In other words, he would get bored, and eventually he will give up. This is an example of a gradient being too shallow. Now, let us take the wheels off and begin by holding the bike, then slowly start releasing the bike so that he gets used to it, and eventually he will be riding the bike all by himself. This example shows a good gradient for learning. Keep the gradient at a pace that fits his or her comfort level, and learning will be at its optimum.

The next step in learning any topic is to practice what you learn consistently until you feel comfortable using it. This can be very difficult if you are without the tangible object or subject you are studying. This is called absence of mass, where we are learning a topic or a subject that is not in front of us or in our presence. This can lead to learning difficulties, and it is best if we can learn in front of or in the presence of that which we are trying to learn. In other words, if we are learning about cars, it is best to learn about cars in the presence of cars. If we are learning about abstract items, like accounting, it is best that we learn accounting by using accounting in real ways. The point is that we must consistently use the knowledge we gain in actuality if we are truly going to learn at levels of true understanding.

Learning by using actual practice is called practical learning, where a person is actually doing as he or she learns. This is so important in learning, and if you can do one thing to improve your ability to learn, this would help tremendously. This is why those who have experience in a subject tend to know the subject better than those who have only learned it in theory. Most education we experience is in theory. In other words, we often learn without the object in front of us.

At times it may be difficult to learn in the presence of the object, and there are some techniques you can use to replace the object. One way is to use a demo kit. This is a tool that includes general items like paper clips, pencils, rubber bands, and the like. Using these items to demonstrate what you are learning allows you to get your actions in on the topic and allows you to learn it more effectively.

For example, you could use these items to represent the parts of a copy machine when learning how to use a copy machine. You could also use pictures and videos, but these are not as effective. In short, try to use what you learn as you learn on the actual object or by doing, and you will learn more effectively.

Another important factor when it comes to learning is that we should always learn material with the idea in mind that we are going to teach the material to someone else. If you are studying a subject that you believe you already know or believe you don't need to know, you can pretty much write the subject off as something you're not going to learn. Learning material with the idea that you are going to teach it gives the material new meaning in that it motivates you to truly try to understand the material at its deepest level, since you will be teaching another person this material later on. In fact, you should actually teach the material to someone like a spouse, friend, or even a stranger to help internalize the knowledge. Teaching gives you the ability to internalize the material, and this is a great way to study. Find a partner who is working on the same course or someone studying another topic, and trade services by teaching each other what you are studying. However, learning a topic to teach it only gives you the ability to learn it at deeper theoretical levels and does not give you the practical knowledge needed to really understand it unless you include practical and actual experience as part of the teaching process. For this reason, when you teach a topic, teach it using the practical method of getting your student in the mass of the topic.

Another area that has been missing in our education is the ability to know how our brains function. There is great truth to the idea that if you truly want to know a topic, you should try to know how it works as well as knowing the steps in using the knowledge to get the outcome of using that knowledge. It is not imperative to know the structure of a subject in order to use it; however, the more we can understand the thing or concept we are learning, the greater our ability to truly know what it is we are learning. We can learn the steps to any process and get by just fine, but if we want to teach the subject and figure out new ways to understand it, it is best to also know structure. Structure can help in that our ability to know why we do something creates greater confidence in our use of the subject. For example, when you learn to fly an airplane, it is not essential to know how a wing helps it to fly, only that you know how the controls work to make the wing do what you want it to do. However, if you understand Bernoulli's principle, you will become more confident in what the wing is capable of; therefore, you will be able to operate the fullest envelope of the airplane's capabilities.

Our brains function in specific ways, and this is another area that our education system has failed us. Memory is an important aspect of knowledge in that it allows us the ability to memorize data so that we can organize the data in ways we can understand it at deeper levels. Simply, we must be able to remember what we read if we are ever going to be able to understand it. Memory is a very specific skill and requires very little effort if you understand how the mind works--specifically, how memory works. When I was young, I had no idea how to memorize information, and I became very frustrated when I was given a great deal of information. I spent many years researching and developing memory techniques, and I have formulated a specific memory program that can help you develop your memory to levels you never dreamed possible.

I spend a great deal of time on memory in this program, because it is a very important topic, but I want you to remember that memorizing data is not learning unless you are able to apply the material and understand each application of any step in the process of using knowledge for its intended use. Use this memory system consistently, and I guarantee you will be able to develop the ability to remember anything you desire, which will help you develop another tool to gain usable knowledge. You will amaze yourself and your friends, and I guarantee you that using this system can improve the quality of your life. If you are a student, your grades will soar if you apply all these learning skills we have talked about. If you are a salesman, you will be able to remember names and important information about each individual you come in contact with. You will be able to remember tasks with greater accuracy than if you wrote them down.

Writing tasks down can often lead to lower performance in that it makes you forget about the task, and most of the time we procrastinate about doing the task, because we relaxed our minds on the task when we put it on paper. This brings me to a very important point: when we write a task down, we simply create a way to remove the task from our minds; therefore, we forget about it altogether. We do this especially with tasks related to crises, because it allows you the ability to forget about the problem temporarily.

I do want to say that writing tasks down is not all bad. For example, it would allow you to leave the worry of the task to another time if it is causing great stress, but once you learn the memory system I present here, you will be able to tuck a task away until you want to deal with it. Remembering a task is different in that it motivates you to deal with it. When you develop your memory, you'll have the ability to know a list of tasks you need to do, and you'll be more likely to complete the tasks, since they are not dumped onto some piece of paper. Without any further ado, let us now take a deeper look at the concept of memory and how it works.

Memory is a skill we all want and can use to better our survival on all eight dynamics and in all areas of life, including our spiritual, physical, mental, emotional, social, service, and leadership aspects, as well as in the roles we play. Memory is not just a skill to be used to remember erroneous data; it is used to remember data that will improve the quality of your life and the lives of others. The knowledge that we should focus on is knowledge that gives us the ability to develop our wisdom, skills, creativity, and ability to act. It is what I call specialized knowledge.

Specialized knowledge supports our survival and moves us toward creative thought. You will learn how to remember anything, including abstract concepts, foreign language, names and faces, numbers, and much more. The bottom line is that this memory system will give you the tools to improve your learning capabilities a thousand-fold. I will prove this in just a moment, but for now trust me on this--you will amaze yourself and your friends when you understand the system given here. I want to make sure you understand that this system was developed based on the way our minds work, so it will be natural and easy to use; in fact, it will become automatic, and for this reason I want to stress a very important point: trust your memory.

Plato once said, "All knowledge is but remembrance." Cicero said, "Memory is the treasury and guardian of all things." No one will argue the importance of memory and the benefits that come about when a person has a memory that most people envy. Whether we are in business or athletics, a strong memory can be an important factor that allows a person to prosper. Most important, in school or in life a good memory can make a world of difference by creating the confidence that is required to succeed.

Memory can be defined as, "the mental function of retaining information about stimuli, events, images, ideas, etc., after the original stimuli are no longer present" (Reber 1995). I have been interested in memory--specifically, the development and improvement of memory--for quite some time. I have studied scholarly research and have read and taken many courses on memory improvement and have learned that a good memory does not have to belong to a genetically gifted individual. A good memory can be owned by anyone willing not only to learn how memory works, and to learn techniques that help one to remember, but most important to act on this newly acquired knowledge.

Memory has been an interest for many people throughout the ages. For example, mnemonics is not a new technique; in fact, it was derived from a name of a Greek goddess, Mnemosyne. The sad truth is, even though memory systems have been around since Greek civilization, memory systems and techniques are not widely used consciously. As you will see, a trained memory is not that difficult to attain, and, hopefully, after reading this section you will be well on your way to the benefits that surface from a trained memory.

To give you confidence of the memory you will acquire by reading and applying this section, I would like to start with a memory test. I would like to give you a list of fifteen words that I will ask you to read once. Please only take two minutes to do so, and then without looking at the list try to remember the list of words in order. Are you ready?

table
speaker
cd
tree
guitar
TV
book
cup
toe
outlet
ceiling
ski
shoe
lamp
briefcase

Another test I would like to administer is a list of items numbered from one to twenty. In this test please take three minutes to try and memorize the items in and out of order. In other words, remember the item and the number it has attached to it. With this test I will show you that memory can also be improved when dealing with abstract items like numbers. Are you ready?

1. beanbag
2. car

3. pencil
4. dictionary
5. class
6. shovel
7. clock
8. piano
9. dog
10. moon
11. rack
12. lift
13. storage
14. closet
15. smoke
16. pool table
17. hat
18. glove
19. pig
20. stapler

How did you do? Don't feel bad if you were only able to get a few of the items on each test, as this is normal for an untrained memory. I can assure you that after reading and applying the information that will be presented, your memory will surprise you. Be sure to keep track of your scores on these tests, because at the end of the section when your memory is trained, your scores will increase tremendously--you will probably get 100 percent.

The physiology of memory will give us an idea of how memory works. For many years, the physiological basis of memory has been of interest to many neuroscientists. One study revealed that memory could be transferred from one flatworm to another (McConnell 1962). In this study, RNA (ribonucleic acid) was transferred from trained worms to untrained worms, where the trained worms had been conditioned to respond to light. In this study, McConnell believed that chemists would be able to develop medications that would facilitate learning of a specific subject. These studies have since been difficult to replicate, which proves we are far from understanding the chemical workings of memory (Weiten 2002). In the future, medicines may be developed that transfer knowledge, but this appears to be far off.

There is evidence that some chemical substances may improve memory. One of these, estrogen, has been linked to an increase in cognitive ability, mainly learning new tasks, and the development of short-term memory. In one study, performed by Richard Mayeux and colleagues, a thousand women aged seventy and up were followed. This study showed that the women who took estrogen for a one-year period were significantly less likely to develop Alzheimer's disease than those who had not taken the hormone at all. It was estimated that women who take estrogen for ten years could possibly reduce the risk of Alzheimer's by 40 percent. It is theorized that estrogen stimulates neurons in the brain to grow more branches (Greider 1996).

Another chemical substance that showed promising effects was anti-inflammatory agents. Our body has a tendency to react against inflammation, which can cause cells to die. Patients who suffer from arthritis showed lower incidences of Alzheimer's disease, and it is believed that patients who have arthritis are more likely to take anti-inflammatory drugs, which may help in reducing the incidence of Alzheimer's (Greider 1996).

The brain is very complex, but researchers have been able to shed some light on the structures of the brain that are involved in the process of memory. Researchers at the University of British Columbia looked at seventeen related studies and found that people taking an anti-inflammatory medication reduced their risk of developing Alzheimer's by nearly 50 percent (Greider 1996). These are just a few examples of how chemical substances can have a positive effect on brain function. The importance of the effects chemicals can have on the brain can be seen on the negative side as well--for example, with marijuana.

There are three questions that are often asked by professionals studying memory: (1) how does information get stored into memory? (2) how is information maintained in memory? and (3) how is information retrieved from memory? Three processes can help in answering the above questions. With regard to question one, how information gets into memory, we should consider the process of encoding. With regard to question two, how information is maintained in memory, we will consider the process of storage. Finally, with regard to question three, how information is retrieved, we shall consider the process of retrieval.

What is encoding? Encoding is the formation of a memory code (Weiten 2002). What is storage? Storage is maintaining encoded information in memory over time (Weiten 2002). What is retrieval? Retrieval is the process in which information is recovered from memory storage (Weiten 2002). This process can be compared to that of a computer. With a computer we have three basic components: a keyboard, a hard drive, and a display monitor. The keyboard can reflect the concept of encoding. It is the tool used to enter information into the hard drive for storage. The hard drive is the storage portion, where encoded information is entered for retrieval at a later date. The monitor is likened to retrieval, where stored information can be displayed.

Encoding is the first step in the process of remembering a thing. There are three aspects of encoding that will be considered: the role of attention, the levels of processing, and the enriching of encoded data. For a person to remember anything it is imperative that the person focuses his or her attention on the data to be remembered (Craik et al. 1996; Mulligan 1998). Attention can be defined as a narrowed focus on a stimuli or event (Weiten 2002). Some psychologists refer to this as selective attention. We can compare attention to that of a filter. A filter allows only certain material to pass through to the next point of destination. Attention allows only that material that has been focused on to enter into the next level of process.

Much debate has been generated as to where attention is applied within the information processing system. Is the information looked at in the early stages, where the information is filtered before meaning is processed? Or has it been considered later in the process, where filtering occurs after the processing of meaning? These two early and late selection considerations have been developed into models of attention labeled as early selection or late selection. As with many ideas, argument usually consists of one theory containing the correct answer, but evidence suggests with this concept that both early and late selection, and possibly an intermediate selection, can be responsible for attention placement (Cowen 1988; Johnston and Dark 1986). This has led many theorists to place a flexible label on attention filter placement (Johnston and Heinz 1978; Shiffrin 1988).

The processing of information should also be considered in search for a general theory of memory. People have a tendency to process information in different ways. This can be seen when one person focuses attention on one aspect more so than another aspect, and another individual reverses their attention intensity to the same aspects. The problem that can occur is the possibility of attention not being focused on the more effective processing scheme. Information can be processed at different levels, and one must consider the effectiveness of each level. Craik and Lockhart (1972) suggest that when considering verbal information people engage in three progressively deeper levels of processing. These include structural, phonemic, and semantic encoding, with structural being a more shallow process, phonemic less shallow, and semantic containing deep processing attributes.

Structural encoding looks at the physical structure of a stimulus. For example, is a word written in bold print, capitalized, or italicized? With phonemic encoding emphasis is placed on what a word sounds like. For example, do two words rhyme? Semantic encoding looks at the meaning of verbal input, like how a word fits in a sentence (Craik and Lockhart 1972). This theory--known as the levels of processing theory--suggests that longer-lasting memory codes are the result of deeper levels of processing (Craik and Lockhart 1972). This idea has been shown in several studies (Koriat and Melkman 1987; Lockhart and Craik 1990).

We can also consider other enrichment dimensions, with regard to the encoding process, to improve memory. With elaboration, one links the stimulus to a time of encoding. This can be seen through examples that explain an idea by way of comparison (Weiten 2002). It is suggested that self-generated examples are best in enhancing memory (Weiten 2002).

Another way to enhance memory is through visual imagery. When one involves himself in the creation of an image in the mind's eye of something to be remembered, an enrichment of encoding may be experienced (Weiten 2002). It has often been said that we think in pictures. An example of this can be seen when the word "elephant" is processed. In general, we typically see the elephant-- that is, the animal--and not the word. We must also consider abstract concepts. It may be that we can remember images of non-abstract origin easier than that of abstract origin (Paivio 1969), which leads us to believe that we are visual creatures. It is also suggested that visual imagery enhances memory, because it provides a second type of memory code. Allen Paivio (1986) developed a dual coding theory in his support of the above concept. This theory states that forming semantic and visual cues will enhance memory recall.

The second key process in memory is that of storage. Three storage capacities will be considered. They are sensory memory, short-term memory, and long-term memory. Sensory memory is the preservation of information in its sensory form for a brief period of time (Weiten 2002). It is believed that visual patterns, sound, or touch have a short-term memory, which allows for the item to be remembered to be present within that sensory avenue. For example, with vision the image we see may actually be an after-image (Weiten 2002). This suggests that sensory memory holds a sensory image, which gives additional time for recognition. This would prevent information from becoming obsolete prior to the information reaching short-term memory.

The second storage capacity is short-term memory. Short-term memory, as defined in the Penguin Dictionary of Psychology, is "Memory for information that has received minimal processing or interpretation" (Reber 1995). Short-term memory holds information for approximately twenty seconds (Wickens 1999), unless it is rehearsed. One can prevent information from being lost in short-term memory via rehearsal, which is the repetition of the information to be remembered, either verbally or cognitively. A study showed proof of the rapid loss of memory when rehearsal could not be exercised. Three consonants were given to a group of undergraduates who were prevented from rehearsing the material by forcing their attention toward another task. This study showed that the participants' memories were accurate for fifteen seconds (Peterson and Peterson 1959). Other studies show even less retention with regard to time (Badley 1996). One must consider, though, interference and the role it played in the loss of information. In fact, cause was usually assigned to time-related decay, but research has shown interference as playing a role also (Cowan et al. 1997; Nairne, Neath, and Serria 1977). The important thing to remember is that the rehearsal process is important, and is required for new data to be processed into long-term memory (Fahey and Santos 2002).

We must also consider short-term memory capacity. Miller (1956) noticed that most people could only remember seven items when the person was attempting to recall unfamiliar material. It is believed that new information causes previous information to be discarded, and is one reason that we can usually remember only six to nine items.

We can increase our short-term capacity by "chunking" material (Simon 1974). With this technique, groups are separated, with each group containing familiar objects, which are then stored as a single unit.

We must also consider working memory. Research has uncovered anomalies with the short-term memory model (Nairne 1996; Neath 1998). With this in mind, short-term memory is more than rehearsal, and attention has been given to a more complex model called working memory (Badley 1989; 1992). Three components should be considered: rehearsal loop, visual spatial sketchpad, and the executive control system. We exercise rehearsal loop when repeating information over and over, such as a phone number to be remembered. The second component, visual spatial sketchpad, allows us to change visual images within our mind's eye in order to see an outcome without actually completing the task, for example, the arrangement of things in a house. The executive control system is used in reasoning and decision making, which provides a way of measuring scenario outcomes.

The third key process in the memory cycle we will now consider is long-term memory. Long-term memory can be defined as an unlimited capacity store that can hold information for long periods of time (Weiten 2002). With this in mind, one view says information in long-term memory is permanent (Weiten 2002). If a person cannot retrieve the information, it is because he or she is unable to find the stored memory. An example is losing your sunglasses--you know you have them, you just don't know where to find them. Another view says that information that cannot be remembered is lost information. An example is sunglasses you never had. The problem with this view is if we are unable to find the information, how would we have ever known it was there to look for in the first place?

For proof that long-term memory storage retains information permanently, we can consider flashbulb memories. These are recollections of momentous events that are vivid and detailed (Brown and Kulik 1977). An example of a flashbulb memory would be our ability to remember what we were doing, how we felt, and where we were on 9/11.

Hypnosis is another way of supporting permanent long-term memory. People under hypnosis often recall childhood events with remarkable detail, when before hypnosis the person was unable to remember much in that time period. Spiegel and Spiegel (1985) suggest that our inability to retrieve information can be attributed to poor retrieval techniques. It should be noted that flashbulb memories and the use of hypnosis should not be considered concrete evidence for the permanent aspect of long-term memory. One study showed that flashbulb memories are not as accurate as other memories (Neisser and Harsch 1992). They are much like regular memories and lose detail over time (McCloskey 1992; Weaver 1993). With regard to hypnosis and recall, accuracy also has been shown in studies to be less than perfect (Dubreuil, Gary, and Loftus 1998; Lynn et al. 1997).

Retrieval is the process by which information is brought out of long-term memory and used for a specific purpose. Recall, as it is otherwise known, under most circumstances requires little effort. However, this is not always the case. To retrieve some information it is helpful to use memory cues. We have all experienced the phenomenon known as "tip of the tongue," which is our inability to remember something we know with the feeling that it is only just out of reach. This is an experience that most people are subject to on average of once a week (Brown 1991). The tip of the tongue phenomena is a good example where retrieval cues may be helpful. Retrieval cues are simply stimuli that help us access information that is needed. An example of this is when something is forgotten and something else reminds us of the forgotten information with the typical response of "Oh, that reminds me."

Another cue that can aid in retrieval is placing ourselves back in the context of a specific event that we are trying to remember. Context cues have been shown to be effective in the retrieval of information (Smith 1998). This can be seen when we are placed in a familiar setting from long ago and the context--that is, the old familiar place--helps to retrieve past memories. This technique is often used within legal investigations to facilitate eyewitness recall (Chandler and Fisher 1996).

Some problems can occur when information is pulled from long-term memory. One such problem, misinformation effect, occurs when subjects recall an event after they have been presented misleading post-event information and the eyewitness account is altered based on the erroneous information presented (Weiten 2002). One study provided evidence that the use of biased information can lead a participant to see information that is not there (Loftus and Palmer 1974). In this study, a group was shown a videotape of a car accident. The participants were then interviewed and asked to give eyewitness testimony. Biasing information was introduced in how the questions were formed. One group was asked how fast the vehicles were going when they hit each other. Another group was asked a similar question, but instead of using the word "hit," the word "smashed" was used. When the subjects were asked to recall what they saw and whether they remembered seeing broken glass, the subjects who were asked the question in terms of "smashing" into each other were more likely to recall broken glass. Those who were presented the question with the words "hit each other" were less likely to see any broken glass. It should be noted that the videotape of the automobile accident showed no evidence of broken glass at all, which points us to consider the possibility of suggestion.

What causes the misinformation effect? One factor, called source monitoring, has to do with the origin of the memories. Source monitoring is considered a main contributor to mistakes made by people while reconstructing their experiences (Johnson 1996; Johnson, Hashtroudi, and Lindsey 1993; Lindsey and Johnson 1991). When a person is asked to provide a specific memory and it is believed that the memories are not tagged to a specific source, errors may be made in source identification, which is referred to as a source monitoring error. For example, did I hear that from a friend, or did I see it on TV? It should be noted that source monitoring errors are backed by confidence about authenticity by the revealer, when in actuality the recollection was inaccurate (Lampinen, Neuschatz, and Payne 1999). An error in retrieval can also be linked to forgetting.

Forgetting can have many causes, including a deficiency in the encoding process, in the storage of the information, in the retrieval of the information, or possibly a combination of these.

Ineffective encoding may point to the fact that some information that has been forgotten never existed in memory in the first place. This is called pseudoforgetting, which is usually because of poor attention (Weiten 2002).

Decay can also be a contributing factor. With this theory, we forget information because of memory traces fading with time (Weiten 2002). However, research has not been able to support decay as a contributing factor in long-term memory forgetting (Slamecka 1992). When considering decay, we would assume that the passage of time would be a significant factor, but it is now believed that more influence and attention should be given to the amount, complexity, and type of information to be assimilated during times of retention. In other words, one must consider interference.

Interference suggests that information is forgotten because of competition of other information. Interference has been shown to be a major influence when considering the loss of information (Anderson and Neely 1996; Bjork 1992). Two kinds of interference should be considered: retroactive and proactive. Retroactive interference occurs when new information retards the retention of old information. With proactive interference, previously learned data retards the retention of new data. Both types of interference are believed to disrupt retrieval (Tulving and Psotka 1971).

We also may forget material because of retrieval failure. In fact, it is believed that a breakdown in the retrieval process is a major contributor to the forgetting of information. Retrieval cues may be the contributing factor. A poor retrieval cue can break down the process and retard retrieval of information. A good retrieval cue will allow for accurate recollection (Tulving and Thompson 1973).

One other factor that should be considered is that of motivated forgetting. We often forget things because we don't want to remember them, as they may have been painful, unpleasant, or embarrassing. Therapists work on retrieving these memories, which Freud believed were blocked by unconscious avoidance tendencies (Freud 1901). Freud termed motivated forgetting repression, which is the suppression of distressing thoughts and feelings into the unconscious. It should be noted that people have had more difficulty remembering information attached to anxiety-laden events, while events that are considered emotionally neutral were more readily recalled (Guenther 1988; Reisner 1998). Little support has been given to the concept of repression specifically (Holmes 1990), but it seems as though repression does have its roots.

Another aspect when considering problems that can occur in the retrieval of memory is aging. Studies have reported a decrease in the elderly and their memory abilities (Baltes and Kliegl 1992; Hultsch and Dixon 1990). It has been shown, though not universally (Shimamura et al. 1995), that there is a decrease in memory within the elderly for prose, television shows, conversations, past activities, and personal plans (Kausler 1995). Speed in learning, solving problems, and processing information are the first aspects of memory that are affected in the elderly (Salthouse and Babcock 1991). This may be a result of physiological changes and neurological functioning (Cerella and Hale 1994; Myerson et al. 1990). It has been shown, however, that many elderly people can maintain a highly functional and superior memory (Simonton 1990).

Two studies show that stereotypes often alter judgments of the elderly and change their cognitive performance. The first study created positive stereotypes of the elderly, which showed improved memory performance, memory self-efficacy, and views of aging within this population. This study also showed negative stereotypes of the elderly, such as worsened memory performance, memory self-efficacy, and the views of elderly among the aging. Elderly people tend to report feeling a loss of memory abilities (Hertzog, Dickson, and Hultsch 1990).

Most everyone is susceptible to the influences of stereotyping, unconscious generalizations that enter a person's mind and that may seem irrelevant to the individual (Langer 1989). An example of this, in relation to an environmental cue, is the sound of an old person's voice, which leads some to activate the use of age stereotypes (Giles, Coupland, Williams, and Nussbaum 1992). It is obvious that outside influences can affect a person's confidence, which can lead that person in the direction of the influence being presented. It would be interesting to do a study on memory techniques in the elderly to see if these techniques can help enhance the performance and capabilities of an elderly mind.

The real question seems to be, how do we get information from its conception into long-term memory and develop the ability to retrieve that information at will? The first and most important aspect of memory is deeply connected to interest in the subject to be learned. We tend to focus more intensely on information that is interesting to us and wander when information seems to serve no purpose.

It is obvious, especially with education, that there is always going to be information that does not interest us all the time. So the first thing we must do is figure out for ourselves how to make uninteresting subjects interesting. One technique I like to use is the challenge that learning provides. In other words, if I can apply memory techniques, a subject that interests me, regardless of the subject being studied, that information becomes relevant. In order to learn something, we must focus our attention on what it is we are trying to learn. We must focus on the stimuli, or event, in such a way that it narrows our attention to that information. Psychologists call this selective attention (Weiten 2002).

There are many memory techniques that can be beneficial in the development of a good memory, one of which is loci. This idea dates back to early Greece, 86-82 B.C. (Yates 1996), and involves using familiar paths and associating items to be remembered with certain locations along this path (Weiten 2002). For example, if you want to remember a list of items, you can attach these items to objects you are familiar with around your house. Another memory technique is the narrative method (Weiten 2002 and Lorayne, 1990). This method creates a story that places the items within the story, which can increase the meaningfulness of the items to be remembered. This is similar in effect to how rhymes work, which are another mnemonic device (Weiten 2002).

Another system is called the link method of memory (Lorayne 1990), which involves linking items together to be remembered, as in the case of a shopping list. For example, a typical list might look like this: eggs, apples, salad, milk, coffee, aspirin, dog food, pop, chicken, and dental floss. The first thing to do would be to remember eggs. This would be the most difficult item to remember, unless you link it to something that will remind you of eggs--for instance, when putting your shoes on, you could link it to visualizing an egg in your shoe. As you put your shoe on, you feel the egg crush under your foot. This brings me to an important aspect of memory. In order to remember a thing, you must see it in your mind's eye and make it ridiculous with great detail--in the case above, you must actually feel and hear the egg crush under your foot (Lorayne 1990).

Now that you have remembered the first item on your list, eggs, the next item to remember is apples. A way to remember this is to see a chicken laying hundreds of apples instead of eggs. See this picture in your mind's eye. The next item is salad. You could picture biting into an apple and instead of the crunchy yellow substance within an apple, there is salad. To help facilitate this memory, not only should you see the salad within the apple, you should also imagine feeling the texture of the salad instead of the apple. The more detail you can add to your picture, the greater chance you have of remembering the items (Lorayne 1990). Try this method with the test items listed at the beginning of the section.

Some will say that the link technique will work only for non-abstract items, but that is simply not true. To remember anything, it must be associated with something we already know (Lorayne 1990). Abstract items can be remembered as long as those items are made familiar. Numbers are a good example, which brings us to the next memory technique, the peg system of memory (Lorayne 1990).

The peg system of memory allows you to remember items in and out of order, that is, by number. Harry Lorayne devised a system called the numeric alphabet. This system allows you to turn numbers into words by attaching a consonant sound to the numbers 0 thru 9. With these consonant sounds, we can make words that will represent any number we want to remember, and then link that word to an item to be remembered. This may sound tedious, but once you understand and practice the concept, applying it will not be difficult at all.

Again, with the numeric alphabet each number to be remembered will have a trigger. Remembering it will be easier, because something about the number will remind you what the sound for that number is. Let's start with the number 0. Zero has the consonant sound of Z or S. The way to remember this is that the word "zero" starts with the consonant sound Z. The next number is 1. The consonant sound for 1 is T or D. The way to remember this is that T can be viewed as two number 1's, one on top of the other. The next number to attach a consonant sound to is 2; the consonant sound for 2 is N. The way to remember this is that the lowercase n has two downstrokes. Next comes the number 3, and the consonant sound for 3 is M. The way to remind you of this is to remember that the letter M has three downstrokes. Number 4 has a consonant sound of R. You can remember this by saying "FOUR" emphasizing the "R" like a golfer says "fore" when he or she hits a ball into the next fairway. Five has a consonant sound of L. This can be remembered by holding your left hand up (showing five fingers) and seeing the L shape made by your index finger and thumb. Six has a consonant sound of SH or J. To remember this, the number 6 turned in reverse looks like a backward J. The sound for 7 is K or the hard C, or G. You can remember this by seeing two number sevens, one right side up and the other upside down. The sound for 8 is F or V. The cursive lowercase f looks like an 8. The sound for 9 is B or P. Remember this by seeing the letter P as a backward 9 (Lorayne 1990).

In order to remember the sounds, you must associate the number with something you already know. This should show you how important association is to memory. Now that you know the numeric alphabet, we can teach the rest of the peg system, which shows you how to make numbers into words, for example, the number 1 has a sound of T or D. We can use the word "tie" as a peg and so your peg word for 1 is "tie." Notice that vowels are freebies, and they are used to make a word. Just to show you how this can be used, I will teach you the first twenty peg words. Then you can apply it to the test words I gave to you at the beginning of the section and memorize them in and out of order. The peg words are:

    1 = Tie
    2 = Noah
    3 = Ma
    4 = Rye
    5 = Law
    6 = Shoe
    7 = Cow
    8 = Ivy
    9 = Bee
    10 = Toes
    11 = Tot
    12 = Tin
    13 = Tomb
    14 = Tire
    15 = Towel
    16 = Dish
    17 = Tack
    18 = Dove
    19 = Tub
    20 = Nose

Notice, these words can only represent the number they are attached to, for example, Ma can only mean the number 3, and Cow can only mean the number 7. Now let's apply this system to our test list. The eighth word on the test list is "piano," and if you want to remember that "piano" is the eighth word, you can picture in your mind's eye a piano made with ivy. You could see yourself playing a piano with keys made of poison ivy, not the usual ivory. See and feel the picture; your hands are itching from the poison ivy. Now, when someone asks you what number 8 on the list is, you will have no problem remembering, piano.

One helpful hint in improving your memory is to try to "see" in your mind's eye the item to be remembered (National Research Counsel 1991). For example, if I say the word "elephant," and you know what an elephant is, you picture the animal, not the word. This is more difficult in remembering abstract items, since you cannot see, for example, the word "air." The ability to see in the mind's eye items to be remembered can increase performance dramatically (National Research Counsel 1991), not only in memory, but in other aspects of human performance as well.

Another hint to improve memory is when you make your images of the items to be remembered, picture them as being ridiculous and out of proportion (Lorayne 1990). An example of this is dreams. Whenever we remember a dream, it is usually a dream in the category of "strange." Most people do not remember logical dreams, but they do remember dreams that create the sense of "that was weird." It is important to get in your picture large quantities of the item to be remembered, which will impress upon your mind a sense of largeness. These are only a few of many techniques that can be used.

There are many ways to improve your memory, and only a few have been touched on within this book. It is now time to go back to the beginning of the chapter and retest yourself on the two tests presented. Before you take the tests again, be sure you understand the techniques presented. I assure you that if you do, you will amaze yourself. Another thing I suggest is to teach this and other memory techniques to your children. I have played memory games with my kids for years and can honestly say it is a major reason as to why they do so well in school. I have been pushing for more emphasis on memory at an early age within our local school system, because I truly believe it can help raise the overall intelligence of our children. Remember, it was Plato who said, "All knowledge is but remembrance."

It's a good idea to make study a habit by setting aside two hours a day for mental growth. Setting aside time to improve such mental capacities such as memory will keep your mind active, and research shows it can improve your physical health as well.

To summarize the Pillars of Excellence learning system, the first step is to always approach the study of any topic with purpose. One must know why they are doing what they are doing, and the reason must be strong enough to motivate the energy for success. Also, study with an open mind; even if you think you know all there is to know about the subject, you can always learn something new. If you think there is nothing else to learn, then try to find a purpose to learn more about the topic, or you may decide that the topic is not for you and move on to something else. There is always something to learn on any subject, so saying that you know it all is really an excuse that says, "This subject bores me."

Try to study with mass so that you are using the material in real, tangible form. Get into the object or concept you are learning, and become an active learner by doing. Study the topic as if you are going to teach it, and for best results actually teach it to anyone who will listen. Never go past a word or a concept you do not fully understand. Get the word understood fully so you can use it yourself in several sentences. In the study of any new area, or even in your area of expertise, familiarize yourself with the vocabulary by getting a dictionary of the subject if one exists. When reading, take one paragraph at a time by first underlining words of the subject, find their definitions, then go back and read the paragraph again, making sure all words are understood. After you understand the paragraph, try to use the knowledge in some way, applying actual activities, demonstrations, or any technique learned here.

Make sure you do not allow yourself to go too fast or too slow. In short, make the gradient appropriate for your speed of learning. Use the memory system as set out in the Pillars of Excellence program, and practice it daily. Study regularly by taking at first a few minutes a day for study, adding a few minutes regularly until you are studying two hours a day. Try to include specialized knowledge in your studies; in other words, study material that will provide you with the ability to improve your life and the lives of others. Most important, learn any topic with the intent to use it, and use it frequently. Finally, as with any activity, we want to make sure we balance our time and energy around that activity so that it gets the full focus it needs. In other words, with education one must be willing to spend a balance of their time studying and actually doing. This allows us to not just learn about a thing, but to actually use it for its intended benefit.

As human beings, we touch only the surface of our mental abilities. Some say this equates to 1 percent, while others say it is more like 10 percent. Either way, imagine what it would be like to use even 15 percent, let alone 100 percent, of our mental capabilities? If we are using on average 10 percent, Einstein would have used 12 percent of his mental capacity, according to some theoretical analogies. This means that as we move up the percentage scale, we will experience some mind-blowing abilities. Einstein was dyslexic, which is a learning disability I had as well. I was told I was disabled, and this affected me for a long time--until I learned how to use my mind. I no longer experience the frustration of being labeled "disabled"; in fact, I am a very gifted student. All I needed was a little faith and the patience of a great teacher to show me how to learn. I had the fortunate opportunity to have a patient teacher, and I hope that is what I can do for you or someone you know who is struggling. The fact is this: if you have a problem learning, chances are you are not any different structurally than anyone else. You have the ability to learn, and all that is needed is a learning system, such as the Pillars of Excellence study technology, to guide you in operating that part of you that separates us from the animal world--our ability to create optimal solutions for optimum survival. Use this system and I guarantee you will be at the top of your class, or at minimum, you will become the intelligent person you have always envied in others. This system works!

I also offer a full seminar on the study technology that many people have used to improve their learning. Many of them bring their kids; in fact, whole families come and enjoy the two days of fun and games that are used to make learning fun. If you or someone you know is suffering from a learning disability or wants to improve learning to higher levels, learn this technology--it will change your life! The seminar offers a way to have fun learning what I've described above, but it can also be done here in this chapter. Understand this chapter and all your learning problems will disappear, and you will be up there with the greatest minds in man's history.

CHAPTER 6

THE EMOTIONAL PILLAR

Emotional intelligence, or EQ, is becoming a very important topic with regard to performance, and it is becoming a major factor in the hiring of employees in corporations around the world. In fact, it is now surpassing IQ (intelligence quotient) for determining the best person for the job. Companies are looking for those with high EQ more so than those with high IQs. I would like to note that a balance of IQ and EQ is better than focusing only on one of these two measures.

Emotions play a big role in life; in fact, we are motivated to seek or avoid certain feelings. This can be narrowed down to the pain-pleasure concept in that we are motivated to gain pleasure and to avoid pain. The pain-pleasure concept is very important in the area of emotions, specifically in state management.

How we feel is directly affected by our emotions, and our emotions are affected by our physiology and our psychology. In the Emotional Pillar you will be guided in developing your emotional intelligence, which is the ability to be self-aware, manage emotions, motivate yourself, understand the emotions of others, and use these skills to develop relationships. To do this we need to define our most common emotions and understand those that give us the power to shape our destiny. You will be taught the emotional tone scale and you will be guided in developing the ability to move up this scale and make real progress. You will learn how to trigger, at will, any state you desire, and you will also be able to affect the emotions of others using specific techniques that work.

To develop emotional intelligence we first need to relieve the negative power of the past. Most of our negative emotions come from our past experiences, which often are the focus of our reality. In other words, these negative experiences are not always what they seemed to be, and it is in these misinterpretations that our experience is affected and we develop negative emotional feelings for a given situation. What we focus on is most real, and I will guide you in developing the ability to see reality from a healthy standpoint. To relieve these past powers is the focus of the first part of the Emotional Pillar. From there we will focus on developing your emotional intelligence using a scale and creating the power of your physiology and psychology to place yourself on the scale at a level of Optimum. To understand emotions, let's first take a look at the concept of the emotionally impaired.

What is emotionally impaired? I would define it as a loss of or decrease in function, specifically in control of emotions (Reber 2001). For example, those who have an internal locus of control believe that what happens to them is directly connected to their own efforts and abilities (Terry 2003). Those who believe that what happens to them in situations or how they behave is not in their control are considered to have an external locus of control; they believe the cause is something other than themselves (Terry 2003). Emotionally impaired people often focus on an external locus of control with regard to their emotional responses.

Our ability to control our states--that is, the emotions we feel-- is one significant way to help the emotionally impaired learn new, more adaptive ways of responding. I truly believe that people want to do one of two things, with regard to emotion. They either want to change the way they feel--that is, happy or confident--or change a behavior, which goes back to how one wants to feel. For example, people who smoke cigarettes and believe that it is unhealthy may have a sense of guilt or concern that causes some anxiety. If the person changes their behavior--that is, he or she stops smoking-- then ultimately a change of state will be experienced; in other words, the reduction of anxiety in the long run. People use drugs, such as nicotine, to change state. However, if they knew how emotions work, they could get the same change in state without having to use nicotine. When a person smokes, they take deep breaths, which changes their physiology, which in turn changes their state. The nicotine and the smoke actually cause them to feel a "high," but only for a short period of time. The deep breathing wakes them up as well, but eventually the nicotine leaves the body and the breathing returns to normal, and the individual is again down. From here they reach for another cigarette and begin the process all over again.

If one were to try taking deep breaths, their state would change and would give their psychology and physiology what they desired. A change in state would occur, and the individual would get the "up" feeling without the danger of the drug and with the benefit of deep breathing. In fact you could perform power breaths where the ratio equals 1:4:2, as mentioned in the Physical Pillar. This means that you would inhale for a count of 1, hold your breath for a count of 4, and exhale for a count of 2. This of course is merely a ratio, so maybe you could try inhaling for a count of 7, hold for a count of 28, and exhale for a count of 14. This will cause a change in state, because you are getting oxygen in abundance. You will also benefit from the healthy benefits of moving lymph fluid, as discussed in the Physical Pillar.

One of the best ways to change how we feel can be done through movement. Movement of the body causes physiological changes. This is especially true for exercise. When a person engages in exercise, breathing and heart rate increase, which causes greater oxygen consumption and blood flow, thus creating extraordinary energy. Another way to control our physiological state is through general activities like cleaning. Cleaning can be very therapeutic; the first thing it does is allow you to control your environment--you end up controlling your environment instead of your environment controlling you. Cleaning also creates motion, which leads to increased oxygen consumption and increased blood flow, which allows the same benefits that regular exercise provides. Cleaning also helps us psychologically, because it puts our focus on something other than our problems and onto something else we can control.

Another way to change state is by controlling our focus, as mentioned above. We often focus on events or situations in our life that we can do nothing about or that we can only do so much to affect. This focus is what is most real to us, so if it is something that causes worry or some form of pain, such as anxiety, that will be your general emotional tone. Focusing on unproductive painful events often takes control of our lives, and it can actually cause the loss of employment or even break up a family, so it is critical that we have a way to change our focus onto something more real and positive. This can be done through interpretation of events--that is, how we define what has happened and what questions we ask ourselves and others. For example, we all know someone who is always in a sense of despair. They ask questions like, "Why does this always happen to me?" This question focuses on the negative, which causes a state of helplessness--in other words, a feeling of loss of control. This can be compared to an external locus of control. What if one were to ask questions like, "What can I learn from this? or "How can I make this meaningful?" I believe these questions force us to look at the positive aspects of a given event. This type of questioning can be compared to an internal locus of control--that is, the individual controls the meaning of the situation by directing their focus on the most productive questions they can think of. In other words, productive questions control their states by directing their focus on positive action, therefore eliminating the power of the negative focus. In short, one can create greater productivity by accepting the situation and finding productive questions that can create an opportunity of growth instead of loss.

Nutrition can also play a significant part in how we feel. For example, a high sugar carbohydrate initially causes an increase in energy, but eventually leads to an emotional crash. Poor nutrition can also cause low blood sugar, which usually expresses itself in such ways as irritability, lethargy, and depression. Following a diet that maintains a steady flow of proper nutrition can help maintain emotional control, because it creates a more stable level in blood sugar, which causes a more stable chemical environment within the body, thus leading to more stable moods.

I cannot remember the last time I felt depressed. Recently I have done much research in the area of state management and have concluded that it is my actions, physically and mentally, that have kept me in peak states. For example, every morning when I wake up I perform a few tasks that change my physiology and my psychology in a direction that supports heightened states like Optimum. The first thing I do is to perform some aerobic exercise. This changes my heart rate and breathing, which causes heightened oxygen consumption and blood flow. During this exercise I also bring in a cognitive aspect. I do this by performing autosuggestions, goal review, mission statement review, gratitude, incantations, and visualization. This directs my focus toward those areas of my life that matter most and takes focus away from the negative aspects.

The program I have developed for raising one's emotional tones is called the GPA Life Cycle. This is basically a process that brings people's states to higher levels on a consistent basis. Most people experience a wide range of emotions throughout the day where they may go from depression to exhilaration and back. This is an example of a person who has lost their ability to manage their states. A person who can manage their states, as is possible by following the GPA Life Cycle, would raise the emotional tone to Optimum and be able to experience Optimum consistently. This is the expectation of the processing of the Emotional Pillar. It should be noted that you will experience an even greater emotional state using the Pillars of Excellence program holistically, bringing all parts of man into the equation.

Throughout the day I also maintain a heightened peak state through deep breathing exercises and by consciously maintaining a positive mental attitude. The positive mental attitude, in my case, is maintained through a sense of love. In other words, I try to project love on everyone, even those who have wronged me. It is amazing how this makes me feel. I also look at life's problems as challenges; if you think about it, life would be rather boring if everything was always easy with no problems at all. Look at the problems you face as challenges; in fact, try to look at life as a game. Take all the challenges you face and keep score, or use the GPA Evaluation technology at the end of each day. To do this all that is required is to grade yourself using the grading system used in school. Give yourself a grade at the end of the day on how you did. You can even make a graph of your grades, which can bring a picture to your experiences and your growth. We use this approach in the personal coaching program, where our clients have a visual picture of their progress.

To help those who are emotionally impaired or those who are looking to improve their emotional intelligence, I would guide them in a direction that supports their psychological and physiological aspects. This can be done through mental focus, nutrition, and exercise. In order to raise our emotions and control them, we must first eliminate those perceptions from the past that control us. These perceptions are experiences we had during moments of depression or other lower emotional tones that get triggered anytime we experience a similar perception. In short, we lose control of our emotions because of past experiences that have caused lower emotional states, and in order to experience greater emotional intelligence, we must remove those things that control our reactions and take control back, to live a more proactive life.

In order to develop our emotional intelligence, we must first extinguish the power of past experiences. These past experiences have left in us triggers that to some extent are controlling the way we react and feel. This is often referred to as stimulus-response and is considered a survival mechanism. The problem arises when we allow these past survival triggers to inappropriately take over. For us to be in control we want to be the cause, and to be the cause we must remove all of the negative stimulus-response triggers. Note: cause is your ability to have an effect on something or someone outside of yourself.

To remove these triggers you can simply apply the following technique. The first step is to go to your earliest memory and write down a word or two that will remind you of the event. Do this as you progress up till your current age and your most frequent memory or event. Now go back to the earliest event and use the words that you wrote down as triggers to remind you of the event, and go over that event several times until you believe you have remembered every last detail you can remember. Include all the perceptions you can, including sight, sound, smell, taste, and all the feelings you can remember, including the pain or the pleasure of the event. This action will bring to your conscious the perceptions that are the triggers for the emotions you felt at the time. Once these triggers are in your conscious, they no longer have the effect on your emotions, because you are in reality--in other words, you separate past from present. Do this with each event until you have covered all the events you can remember. It is important to note that as you do this, events you couldn't remember at the beginning of this process will also reveal themselves. Do the same with these events, and eventually you will have cleared each event and will no longer have the triggers that automatically triggered certain emotions.

It is important to look for indicators during this process that indicate the event is now taken out of the trigger mechanism and into reality. As you go over each event, you will initially experience some pain--at times even extreme pain--depending on the severity of the event and its effect on you. You will also experience pleasure from those events that represented a pleasurable moment, and you may begin to smile or even laugh. The painful events will require you to go over them several times, but eventually you will begin to experience a lift that will feel like a weight has been removed from your body. This will continue until eventually you will be going over the event and all of a sudden the experience will begin to make you smile or laugh. At minimum you will experience a feeling of relief--this is the indicator that the event no longer has control. I would suggest that you take some time doing this so you are not overwhelmed. In fact, one event may take several sessions in order to get it removed, but eventually it will not have power and you can then move to the next event.

During times of pain try to continue, but if it becomes unbearable, let it go for the moment and go back to it as soon as you can. Try to get through the pain, and continue until you get the release and realize that the pain is only temporary, and eventually you will experience great pleasure. If possible, do this with a friend so that both of you are describing your own events to the other person and helping each other remove these powerful triggers. I do not suggest doing this with strangers, since we are less likely to be completely honest with them and may unconsciously hold back our perceptions. Find a friend you can trust and let it all out. If you are not comfortable sharing with someone else, do it on your own. Having a friend will help you through the tough times, but it is not necessary. Once you have covered all events that you can remember, try to think of other events. You will notice that doing this exercise can bring to the surface events you never remembered, so don't be surprised if events continue to reveal themselves. You will eventually get all events covered and attain the release needed to free you of these controlling forces in your life.

It is important to have a sense of the purpose of your life, your life's meaning. We looked at this in the Spiritual Pillar, but I would like to give you some tips on how to recognize what purpose/

meaning your life may have. Many people have problems finding their purpose, because they fail to look in the right place for it. Most of the people who know their purpose and are passionate about that purpose found it in their experience; in fact, they may have found it in their most painful experiences. For example, the woman who started MADD was the mother of a child who was killed by a drunk driver. Imagine the pain and suffering she must have experienced and that many others experience every year because of similar tragedies. However, the only way to live through such an experience is to give it meaning. Now, you may ask, how could someone killing my child have meaning? Well, if you look hard enough, you can find that meaning.

Every experience we have can have great meaning and can provide purpose for our existence. Once you understand this, life becomes much more important. In fact, I would offer that many of those who are suffering from depression are afflicted with a lack of meaning, and if they put meaning into their life, their depression would lift. Look at it this way--the people who have experienced the greatest suffering/pain are those who have the greatest opportunity to experience the most powerful meanings. In the case of the woman who started MADD, she took her child's death and made certain it would not be a wasted death. She vowed to clean our streets of drunk drivers, and she has done a fantastic job. Her child's death means something, and it provided the benefit to others and saved thousands, maybe millions, of lives. Of course it would be better to have the child alive, but there is nothing that can be done to bring her back. The best way to keep the child alive is to allow her death to make a difference for mankind.

Suffering is often where we find our greatest purpose in life. Victor Frankl, a Jewish man who survived the death camps of Germany, developed Logo therapy, which basically allows us to find meaning in life. Logo therapy guides you to look at suffering in a new way, by allowing you to bring meaning from pain. It also allows the ability to look at what you have been through and see your experience as an education and a training ground for what you are meant to do. One way to do this is to find meaning in our suffering. Many may think this is crazy, but if you look at some of the most influential people of history, you will find they begin their greatest achievements with suffering. It is what got them to where they went and gave them the fuel to make a difference. I have seen this idea work miracles, and I promise if you can find meaning in your suffering and purpose in your past, you will live a more powerful life.

In many situations a person who has experienced great suffering will never be able to live life without depression unless they find meaning in their suffering. I truly believe that a great deal of depression stems from similar situations. A person is depressed because their life lacks meaning and they find no joy in anything they do. If the person could help others find solutions to life's issues, using the experience they have from their own suffering, it can become not only therapeutic, but it can also pave the road ahead and give them a life they would never had experienced if they did not suffer. I would offer that if you want to find the life you have wanted, it will best be found in your suffering and experiences. Most people never live the life they dreamed of, because they never looked at their experiences as a training ground for the work. This is because many people want to avoid pain, and when we look at the past, especially the painful past, we want to ignore it, so we never really try to understand it. Once you get the courage to look at your painful past, you will truly start to live. Look at it from many angles, and try to find out how that experience can give mankind a saner place to live. At times this may be difficult, but it will be worth it in the end. The experience can get very personal, so I would suggest that you do this with someone who knows how to deal with emotional pain. We offer this as part of our coaching program; in fact, it is a big part of the process. My of my clients who do this make the turn in life that brings them the meaning they had been searching for.

A great time to do review your past is when you perform trigger therapy. As you are going over your past experiences, look at them from a viewpoint of purpose and meaning. Ask yourself, Why did this happen, and what can I take from this to improve my life or someone else's life? Ask these kinds of questions, and you will start to see a whole new world--the world you were meant to live.

Now that you have removed the power of the past and found reason for your suffering that brings purpose to life, you will move up the tone scale--in other words, you will now experience higher emotional states. This is one of the greatest benefits of my program--to be at emotional tones that generate happiness. You will be able to take control of your emotional states with greater success. To control our states we must be able to control what the past means to us and what the future means to us. This is using our focus, or our psychological aspect, to control our emotions. Another way to help control our states is via physiological aspects. Using psychological and physiological techniques to control states is a great way to live a more fulfilling life. Let's discuss these techniques and get you started on taking back control of how you feel, therefore gaining control of your destiny.

Most of what we are doing is trying to control how we feel. We are behaving in such ways as to bring about a desired emotional outcome. Many scholars believe that our existence is hinged to the idea that all we are doing in life is creating the emotional states that bring pleasure. This is a pretty shallow view, but it offers a bit of insight to some truth. For example, the primary reason that people overeat is because they want to change the way they feel. Have you ever been depressed or just bored and find yourself looking into the refrigerator? The reason this happens is because you want to change your state. This is probably the number one cause of obesity and all the diseases that come with obesity. If you could change your negative state, like boredom, to the positive state of exhilaration without eating or having to do something unhealthy, you would solve a good number of problems in your life. Well, you can learn to change state. You can learn how to take control and attain any state you desire. Don't get me wrong--we don't want to rid ourselves of all emotions except happiness, because that would not be healthy. There is a reason we feel sadness, for example. What I am talking about is being able to experience your emotions with the correct level of response to any given situation and to bring about any desired state you wish.

To be able to change state at will requires EQ, or emotional intelligence. What is EQ? EQ is a person's ability to understand their emotions and the emotions of others. It is a person's ability to recognize whether their response to a given situation is a correct one, or if the emotion they are experiencing is too much, too little, or just right. It can be seen best in the following five criteria:

The ability to know our own emotions. To be self-aware.
The ability to manage our emotional states.
The ability to motivate ourselves.
The ability to recognize the emotional states of others.
The ability to apply techniques to guide others to controlling their own emotions.

These five criteria are not by any means the only criteria--they merely serve as a guide to give us something to work from. We will now discuss each one of these in greater depth to give you a better understanding. To know yourself, to be self-aware, is critical. If you can understand what you are feeling, you are well on your way. In fact, for those who suffer from emotional outbursts, developing self-awareness is usually the fix. The approach here is mainly psychological, but I want to add that physiological approaches work in conjunction with all five approaches, which will be discussed later. As a fix for emotional outbursts, it is important to see this in the following example: if you are someone who suffers from anger, the ability to be self-aware can be the only requirement to remove outbursts that do not match the situation. Our bodies respond to events in such a way that we are ready for survival. In other words, when we become angry we often react in the moment, and if you have ever stopped yourself from getting angry, chances are you began to swell and realized that the situation did not require anger. In short, our bodies react as the initial response, and then our intellect takes over. Those who can't control anger are literally not aware of how they really feel. They are allowing their body to dictate the response. Animals do the same thing, but humans have the ability to determine whether the triggered response is appropriate. Our body gets us moving in the direction for the possible attack, just in case. To control anger, then, requires a person's ability to be aware of their emotions and in turn apply this skill when they feel angry. With those who can't control their anger, it can be said they have no control of their emotional response and are literally responding automatically. This is called an emotional hijacking. When a person can recognize the initial emotional outburst and realize that the situation does not require anger--or at minimum, not so much anger--they take over and control their emotional outburst. The response is amazing, and often this recognition is the cure. This response is true for all emotions, and if you understand this, you are well on your way to emotional intelligence, or state management.

The next important step to increasing EQ is developing how well you manage your states. As mentioned above there are two ways to manage our states. The first is psychological, and the second is physiological. Using the psychological aspect to state management, we must be able to recognize what it is we are feeling. Also, the psychological approach requires the ability to control our focus. We often perceive life in the negative, focusing on the grim possibilities. This leads us to look at life in ways that create lower emotional tones, making us feel fear, sorrow, lethargy, and other low tones. What we perceive, we believe, so if we always look at the bad, we will see life in a bad light. However, if we see and perceive the good, then life seems to be bright and full of color. It is in your control--you choose what to see, so you choose the way it is perceived. Start looking for the positive, and your perception of the world will also turn positive. With regard to the physiological aspect, motion creates in us, like exercise, a euphoric state from the release of endorphins. This makes us feel good, and when we feel good, we tend to look more at the positive than we do the negative.

The next step in developing a higher EQ is the ability to motivate oneself. If you require others--or even the situation--to motivate you, life will control you. If you can motivate yourself, you take control of life and your destiny. Both the psychological aspect and the physiological aspects are important for your ability to motivate yourself. Psychologically, what we focus on can bring either frustration or motivation. If we consistently envision and expect the worst outcome, we will not be moved; however, if we focus on the positive outcome that we desire, it can drive us toward the goal we are after. This is also true in the physiological part. Again, when we exercise we raise our states as a result of greater blood flow, oxygen consumption, and the release of endorphins. Actually, any kind of movement helps do this, but the movement that is best is movement that affects your physical being in a positive way. House cleaning and getting your body fit are two examples. Later we will go over some great technology that will allow you to use both your psychological and physiological aspects at will.

To be emotionally intelligent one must be able to evaluate the emotions of others. In sales it can be said that the success of the salesperson hinges on his or her ability to read another person's emotions. This concept can get tricky, but it is easy if you understand it. Normally we do not listen well to others, because we are formulating our own response rather than listening to what the other person is saying. If we are not paying attention, and even if we are paying attention to the other person's words, we would still have trouble understanding the person's emotional state. We must listen at the deepest level if we want to read their emotions, which requires us to read not only their words but their body language as well. The ability to understand the emotions of others requires us to look at their physiology and psychology.

When people are depressed or are experiencing a lower emotional tone, they usually hold themselves differently than those who are higher up on the emotional scale. When someone is depressed, they slouch and look down. They move slowly and speak in monotone. A person who is higher up on the tone scale holds their body high, head high, and the tone in their voice is elevated as well. This is easy to recognize if you really pay attention. Try it and you will see that you will be able to read another's emotional tones with great accuracy. Notice how you stand, what you are saying, and how you are saying it when you are feeling up, and you will be able to understand the same in others. Look at yourself when you are down as well, and again you will see the truth in emotions and how they can never lie. When you understand the emotional states of others, then you hold the key to the next important step to developing a higher EQ.

The ability to manage your states is very important, but what about managing other people's emotions? This is one of the most important concepts to interpersonal relations. Developing this skill requires a great deal of ethics on your part. Never use it to control others in negative ways. The only reason to use this skill is for their benefit. Managing other people's emotions is really guiding and influencing the other person. It requires the psychological and physiological aspects, and I must point out here that all emotional intelligence requires the use of both psychological and physiological techniques. Both are very effective, but together they are extremely powerful and should always be considered when dealing with emotions.

The trick here is not to try to get the other person from depressed to excited in one move. A person can only move so quickly up the tone scale. The best way is to use the mirroring technique. This requires you to evaluate the other person's emotions and match them. For example, if you are speaking to someone and you notice that they are cynical, you too must at first be cynical. This allows there to be affinity or understanding. The person is going to connect with you. Now, once you have matched the person's emotions, slowly move up the tone scale, which we will cover in just a bit. Watch the person's tones, and if he is not following your lead, go back and try again, only this time move up more slowly. It is important to note that once you match the other person's tone and move him or her up, you will experience a sense of reality together. You will understand each other. Now that you have affinity and reality with the person, you can communicate. Raising another person's emotional tone is an important part of communication. Please keep in mind that in order to do this, you must be aware and use the two emotional tools of the psychological and the physiological. Both the mental and the physical must be paired if you are to be successful at raising another person's emotions.

This is a great tool in all relationships, whether it's marriage, friendships, work-related, or any other type of relationship. For example, in sales we are really trying to meet another person's emotional need. You see this when you are sold something you never needed in the first place--in other words, you purchased with your heart, not your mind. Car salespeople are great at this. They get you to feel a state of freedom, for example, or a state of success, and the next thing you know you are riding home in a Hummer when all you were looking for was a practical minivan for the family.

Advertising is great at using pain and pleasure to entice us to purchase. First they get you into a great state of pain, and then they save the day and give you a great deal of pleasure. For example, a certain credit card commercial portrays a guy on the phone with his mom. His dad just had a heart attack, and his mom is telling him that his father may not make it. The guy gets off the phone and realizes he does not have enough to buy a plane ticket. He calls the credit card company, and they tell him they'll be happy to raise his limit. The card company has saved the day for him and created a pleasurable feeling for you, because the guy now gets to see his dad. We see this in many commercials and even in regular print advertisements.

The above examples are so powerful that sometimes they become unethical. If you want to use these techniques, again, be sure you are not just trying to control another person, but rather teaching them how they can control their own emotions. A good salesperson is trying to improve the condition of the customer, unless that salesperson is unethical. If you use it correctly, you can help the customer by using the pain-pleasure technique or by mirroring them and showing them how good they could feel using your product. The bottom line is to use your ethics and only do good with these tools.

It is important to manage your own states and to help others to do the same. To do this I have developed a technology that you can use to attain any state you desire. Remember, there are two ways to control our emotions: by using psychology and by using physiology. Both require your effort, but eventually the emotions you go after the most will be your chronic emotional tones or the tones that you will be most likely to experience on a regular basis. This is the goal: to create a higher emotional state on a consistent basis.

In many cases the emotions people experience reflect a negative tone; their chronic tone levels reflect negative emotional tones. What I am about to explain will take any negative emotion and replace it with a positive emotion so that you can start to experience whatever emotion you choose. If you choose positive emotions, then eventually you will experience a chronic tone that represents a positive tone. We have a choice of the emotions we want to experience on a chronic level by purposely attaining a positive state. The following two techniques will give you a very powerful tool that can help you define your destiny.

The first tool we can use to control our states is physiological. For example, motion directly affects emotion, because the motion will cause the body to release endorphins that will give you a state of feeling euphoric. If exercise is intense enough and hard enough, one will achieve what is referred to as a "runner's high." In other words, if you are exercising, you will experience higher emotional states or more positive emotional states than if you are just sitting around. For this reason, an exercise program that is consistent--such as the one in the Pillars of Excellence Physical Program--will give you the tools needed in the physiological area to live higher on the emotional tone scale.

Another physiological approach is cleaning; in fact, cleaning can be therapeutic if you are depressed. Cleaning actually helps you control states through two avenues. One way is the physiological motion, and the other is psychological focus and satisfaction. Physiologically, cleaning involves motion, which causes increased blood flow and the release of endorphins. Cleaning also involves the psychological avenue, forcing you to focus on something other than what is causing you to feel down. It also makes you organize your physical universe, which gives you a sense of control. Often one of the reasons we become stressed is that we feel as though we have lost control.

Motion is not the only way our physiology can help us control our states. We can also use our posture. If you are slumped over, like a depressed person holds themselves physically, you will be more likely to experience depression. However, if you stand tall, for example, you will feel powerful and your emotional states are more likely to rise. I call this the Superman stance. Try it. Stand as if you rule the world. Put a smile on your face and try to get depressed. You can't! Now look up to the sky. This was proven to work in a study that had chronically depressed people look into a mirror with a big smile for twenty minutes a day. The results showed that those who did this were more likely to overcome their depression than those who did not. It also showed a difference in moods of the subject just after the exercise, which allowed therapy to be more effective. The key was to get therapy in just after the exercise.

The next way to control your states is through psychological routes. As mentioned above, our focus can help us change states at will. We often focus on those things that are causing stress, which causes us to experience negative emotions quite frequently. What we focus on is most real, so if we focus on the negative, we will experience negative emotions. However, if we focus on the positive, we will experience positive emotions. There is something to be said about positive mental attitudes, or PMA. I do believe PMA works as long as you employ the other techniques as well. Positive mental attitudes cannot change, for example, the trash on the floor of your car, but it can help you see through the trash and into a brighter future. Helping us focus on the positive in life can be achieved using filters. Filters are what we use in order to see the world as we have experienced it. To use the most effective filter, one must understand that a conscious effort must be made in using your intelligence to come up with the most truthful reality. For example, a person who has been robbed by a college student may filter their world by making judgments on all college students by stating that all college students steal. In reality we know this is not true, so we must psychologically realize this and change our perception.

To get yourself to focus on positive aspects it is important to have positive material to focus on. What are the most powerful positive aspects we can focus on that would benefit us the most? Of course it is your future, not your past. At the completion of this program you will have many tools to enhance your life, including the following: your vision, identity, values, beliefs, code of conduct, and more. With these one can develop their GPA Life Cycle, which can be used to raise your tones quickly and effectively. Basically you will implement physiological and psychological techniques that will improve your emotional tones and create a laser-beam focus on the life you desire.

I will now show you one of the most powerful tools that can help you change your life. The activities that I prescribe should be done first thing in the morning, but if that is impossible, then doing them at any time during the day is better than not doing them at all. The benefit in doing them in the morning is that it creates a positive action that will set the tone of your day. In fact, you will experience the zone when you perform these activities, which will stay with you throughout the day and give you that positive start that is needed to experience optimum performance. There is really no reason I can think of why someone can't do this first thing in the morning. Please note that by "morning" I mean the first thing after you wake. If you work nights, then your morning is different, and when you wake, this is the time you should do these activities.

These activities will guide you to raise your emotional tones using a combination of psychological and physiological tools. When used consistently, these activities will bring your emotional tone level up, and eventually your chronic emotional level will rise as well. As soon as you rise out of bed, put on some workout clothes and go outside or hop on any aerobic exercise equipment. Begin your aerobic workout starting with a two-minute warm-up. At the same time, focus on all the good in your life--for example, for your progress in each pillar of your life. Once you have given gratitude for those good things, begin the GPA Life Cycle.

The GPA Life Cycle consists of performing twenty minutes of intense aerobics and combining it with incantations, visualizations, and more gratitude. Your incantations and visualizations should be created using your vision of who you want to become; your personal identity, values, beliefs; and your code of conduct. In fact, try to get as much of your positive stuff into the picture as you can. I could set up a word-for-word program, but that would hinder your progress. Make up your own incantations, your own vision, your own values and code of conduct, and place this together so it brings you motivation and a clear picture of where you are going.

At the completion of this program we will have completed the development of this activity, but for now I want you to begin using it immediately. If you do not have any idea of the values you hold or any of the other material, all you have to do is perform the aerobic exercises and at the same time, with power in your voice, say to yourself: "All I need is within me now . . . All I need is within me now." Do and say this over and over for about two minutes. From here, start to focus on each area of your life and ask yourself, "What is important to me in _____?" For example, what is important to me spiritually? What is important to me physically? What is important to me mentally? What is important to me emotionally? What is important to me socially? What is important for me to contribute? What is important to me as a leader? Ask this question, too, within each of the roles you play; for example, what is important to me as a spouse? What is important to me as a lawyer? What is important to me as a parent?

This exercise will give you the ability not only to change your state, but also to find what you value within each area. Eventually you will know exactly what it is you value in each area, and from there you can create the GPA Life Cycle. In short, for each area of your life you will know what your goal is, the purpose for attaining that goal, and how you will achieve it. In other words, you will know your Goals, Purposes, and Actions--GPA.

When you perform the GPA Life Cycle, the change of state you will experience will be dramatic, and you will begin your day on a powerful positive note. Begin working on developing your vision, your goals in each pillar, and start developing the visual pictures, incantations, identity, and all the other powerful aids that can be incorporated in the GPA Life Cycle. It is your creation, and as long as you get your emotions into it, both physiologically and psychologically, you will create an extremely effective tool for a real life change.

Later I'll talk about parts of the program called the GPA Goal-Setting technology, the GPA Life Management system, and the GPA Life Cycle. The GPA Life Enhancement technologies are the most powerful achievement formulas ever developed. We will cover these parts of the program more deeply in just a bit, but to give you an idea of how we use it in the GPA Life Cycle, I will give a brief description. GPA stands for Goal, Purpose, and Action. If we want to attain anything, we must know exactly what it is we want. In other words, we must have a clear, well-defined goal. Next you must know why you want the goal. This must contain emotion, where the purpose becomes very meaningful. Finally, if you want to attain something, you must develop a plan of action and take consistent action to achieve your goal.

Now that you understand this, you can apply these ideas to your GPA Life Cycle as well. Simply memorize your goals, purposes, and actions, which will be easy using the Pillars of Excellence study technology, and develop incantations or just review them in a positive, upbeat tone. Make sure to envision yourself achieving your goal, feel it, know why you want the goal. Get as much into the picture as you can--feel the exhilaration and all the perceptions that you can. See yourself taking the appropriate actions and how it will make you feel when you make the right choice. Do these with the roles you play--in fact, do it with all areas of your life. If you find that twenty minutes is not long enough to complete your GPA Life Cycle, then go ahead and extend your exercise. However long it takes, do it. It should not take longer then thirty minutes, but I have had times where I really got on a roll and did not finish until I was forty-five minutes into the exercise. It will be worth every minute of your time, and I promise it will pay off.

Use the above technology for state management, and I guarantee you a life that you will be excited about. No longer will you wake up at 6:00 a.m. still tired. You will wake up at 6:00 a.m. ready to start the day with a passion for living and a drive that will make Anthony Robbins look like a depressed man. You will know where you are going, why you are going there, and how you will get there. You will feel a sense of control in your life and a new sense of stability and confidence. Performing the GPA Life Cycle is not only great for changing state in the morning, but its techniques can also be used throughout the day to change any behavior you want to change, to maintain those behaviors you like, and to get a quick state change for that needed extra push in a time of crises. The fact remains that what we do is directly connected to the way we want to feel. The emotions we want to experience are really what we are after. Remember the pain-pleasure principle and how we are looking to create ultimate joy in our life. Joy is an emotion. It is often the cause of addiction. In other words, whenever someone smokes, uses coke, heroin, or just caffeine, they are trying to change the way they feel. They are trying to change state and attain the state of joy. Sometimes the state one is after is something else, such as self-esteem or a sense of meaning. Either way, our actions are somehow an attempt to attain a desired state of emotion.

Changing state is what we are trying to do when we smoke, eat, or perform any activity that changes our physiology or our psychology. With this in mind, try quitting your negative behaviors using your physiology and psychology, and your success rate will be much greater, as long as you really want to quit. For example, instead of reaching for a cigarette, perform some deep breathing exercises. This can be done in the following way: inhale for five seconds, hold for twenty seconds, and release for ten seconds. The ratio in the breathing pattern is 1:4:2. Increase the time intervals as you get stronger--for example, inhale for seven seconds, hold your breath for twenty-eight seconds, and release your breath for fourteen seconds. Apply a psychological technique as well by giving gratitude, incantations, or by reviewing the goals, purposes, and actions for quitting smoking. This will take your mind off the negative behavior and place a more positive behavior in front. The deep breathing and change in focus will change your physiology and your psychology, which will give you the tools to overcome any urge. This technique is so powerful that it can be used to get a heroin addict off of heroin, the most powerfully addictive substance on the planet. I simply apply these techniques, and the addict's cravings subside as they redirect their thoughts onto something more constructive.

As mentioned earlier, we have an effect on others and their emotional states, which is really what relationships are about. Think about all the relationships you have, and you will notice that the relationship is a process of evaluating emotions and acting to enhance, change, or maintain a certain emotional tone. This is seen in sales when we are trying to get another person excited about a product, or at home with our spouse or significant other when we unexpectedly do something nice for them. It is also seen when we are trying to become intimate with another. In fact, the success of any intimate relationship depends on whether each partner meets the other partner's emotional needs. If we can't, the relationship will eventually fail.

Being able to evaluate your emotional states and the emotional states of others, and then having the ability to help the other person attain the emotion they are seeking, is a key factor in the success of all relationships. This is important for many reasons, especially if you deal with people in your business. Emotional evaluation at first can be tricky, since people have a tendency to hide their emotions, but eventually you will get good at it. One way is to use your intuition. You will generally know when another person is unhappy or truly happy. Practice daily; read the emotional tones of everyone with whom you come into contact, and eventually you will never fail at the evaluation and diagnosis of the person's emotional tone and meeting the tone they seek.

Once you are capable of evaluating emotions, you can then change another person's state as quickly and effectively as you can change your own. Simply evaluate the other person's tone and bring yourself to their tone level. This is important because it is difficult to connect or build rapport with another person when you are at a different tone of emotion. We must try to match the other person's tone if we are going to connect. Mirroring another person's state allows you to connect with him or her and build the rapport needed for developing a good connection. Once that initial connection is made, start moving up the emotional tone scale slowly, one or two levels, and watch the other person follow. It happens every time, but it cannot happen if you are not connected. However, if you meet the other person's tone, a connection will occur and you will be able to lift them to higher emotional tones.

Mirroring can be a very effective tool in helping others experience life with a happier, more positive outlook. Another great benefit can be seen in relationships with regard to developing a desire to be with another person. Once the person experiences this higher emotional state that you have guided them to, they will unconsciously associate this good feeling with your presence, and you will find the person wanting to spend more and more time with you.

This is great for all types of relationships--significant others, friends, business, and others. By tuning in to other people's emotional tones, you will be able to develop powerful relationships that are held together and will stand the test that all relationships encounter. Whether we need to develop personal relationships or professional relationships, we need to understand the power of emotions and the ability to guide yourself and others to a desired emotional state.

Our states are affected by others, and we can affect others emotions as well without even trying. In fact, groups tend to reflect the emotional tones that are most consistent of that group. For example, if you belong to a group of highly motivated people, chances are you too will become highly motivated. If the group is negative, if you are not careful, you too will become negative. Emotions are contagious, and we must remember this if we want to be successful. The power of such group tones can be strong, but nothing can match the power of one person who understands the concept of mirroring. You can go into any group and change their chronic emotional tone. In fact, the people who can bring the highest emotional tones to the group will win and are usually the leaders of that particular group. In other words, those who bring a positive tone to the group will overcome those who bring a negative tone.

In order to evaluate emotional tones, we must have a way to label emotional tones. This will give us a guide to refer to and a stable basis from which we can assign tones and find tones we desire. I believe it is best for the individual to develop their own tone scale. However, I'd like to give you an example of a tone scale that you can follow. The scale does not contain all the emotions we can experience, but it gives us a general tone at each level. Following is a scale from 0 to 10 with various emotions attached to each number. The scale is a gradient scale in that the lower numbers reflect negative emotions, and as you move up the scale, they increase gradually into more positive tones. These are estimates of the base emotions, and it is important to understand that a gradual increase of emotions is experienced between each emotion shown. You can apply to this scale any emotion you connect with, as long as they represent emotions similar to those that I have used, since the emotions I have used reflect the general emotions of all human beings, and that the emotions move up the scale in gradient fashion to reflect more positive tones the higher the number. In fact, I highly recommend that you develop your own scale, but for now go ahead and use the scale provided.

This tone scale can be an effective tool in beginning to really recognize your own emotions, and it is a great tool to evaluate the emotions of others. It will guide you in identifying emotions of yourself and others, which is the first step in developing your emotional intelligence.

The emotions are numbered from 0 to 10, with 0 equaling death and 10 representing Optimum, or the state of serenity. By "death" I am referring to emotional death, where the person is at a state of despair emotionally. However, it is important to note that our physical states are in line with our emotional states, and we can read another person's emotions by looking at their physiology. How are they standing? Are they slumped over or standing tall? Are they expressionless or are they smiling from ear to ear? If the person is in despair, they will be slumped over and will have no expression. This is at 0 on the emotional tone scale.

The next emotion on the scale, at the number 1 position, can be considered hopelessness. A person who has a sense of hopelessness shows signs of giving up. These people often give things away, because they lose connection with material goods. They are often suicidal. This is because the person has disconnected from mass; they lack ownership and their physical environment reflects lack of care.

At the number 2 position we see the emotion of anger, where the person becomes uncomfortable with their surroundings and their self. Motion tends to make these people nervous, and any kind of noise, regardless of origin, causes them to react. They are creatures of stimulus response, where reaction is consistent. They do not think before they act, and their behavior reflects that of an animal.

At level 3 we see the emotion of anxiety, where the person cannot stand motion. They get very nervous if activity is not caused by them. They are affected by their environment, and in no way do they have an effect on their environment. They too react to situations without thought.

At level 4 we start to see a shift in which the person no longer shows signs of antisocial behavior. They become more accepting of others, but they are less accepting of themselves. We call this emotional boredom. Physically they are showing signs of life, but they are not energized. These people know that they have the ability to think and to have an effect on their environment--they just don't know how to do it. Their main problem is that they know they have the ability to control their environment but lack the ability to choose the correct response, or should I say they lack the ability to respond with confidence.

At level 5 we meet the halfway point, where a person's emotional state can be interpreted as having mild interest. The person at this level still shows signs of motivation, but lacks drive or the ability to sustain a motivated state. This level is considered to be the median of the average emotional tone in our society and in the general population, and this can explain why today there seems to be less and less innovation and creation. When we are interested in a thing, we are not generally able to act on that interest. We need passion, and a person at this emotional level lacks the passion to make a difference.

At level 6 a person shows a greater interest and perhaps some excitement. These are the emotions we shall strive for, and they begin with the emotion of strong interest. Physically the person is standing taller, and you may even see them smile from time to time. They are not quite consistent in action, but they do what is necessary to achieve what is considered necessity.

Moving up the scale to level 7, we find people with enthusiasm. Here the person has more than strong interest and is actually pushing for that which motivates them. We begin to see that driving force that will allow for consistent action to achieve what they desire. These people complete tasks and enjoy the fruits of their labor. They lack the ability to get other people excited, so this level is not quite ready for the ability to have an effect on others; however, they tend to have an effect on things or material goods.

Level 8 we consider the emotion of eagerness, where the individual is motivated to move in the direction of change. It is where we see the creation of ideas and the actual development of those ideas to reality. We see a person who is confident in stature and who often smiles. They not only affect their environment, but they also have a general pull on others to follow them. They still lack the ability to move all involved to a general outcome, but they can get many people to take some action to the desired end result.

At Level 9 we see the emotion of passion, where the person is living with purpose. They know what they want and they know how to get it. They are infectious and hold a great deal of charisma. They believe they have the ability to make change happen. The one thing they lack is a sense of meaning. They may feel a general tone of meaning, but it fades because the material world still has some pull on them.

The emotion at level 10 is the ultimate emotion, which I call Optimum, sometimes referred to as serenity. Here the individual is happy about life and content with their surroundings. They are always positive and hold a great deal of optimism. They see a great deal of meaning in their life, and they know what they are here for. They are focused on their desire, and all of their actions support the survival of self, procreation/nurturing, the group, mankind, all living things, all nonliving things, spirit, and God. They know that it is up to them to maintain the natural principles, and they know if they do not, they will be affected in a negative way. They are happy with themselves and require no material objects to create happiness. They are in touch with their spirit and they know their life is important.

Emotional Tone Scale	
0 Emotional Death, or Despair	6 Strong Interest
1 Hopelessness	7 Enthusiasm
2 Anger	8 Eagerness
3 Anxiety	9 Passion
4 Emotional Boredom	10 Optimum, or Serenity
5 Mild Interest	

As you can see, these emotions reflect a person's ability or will to live or die. As a person moves up the scale, the will to live becomes very powerful. Knowing these emotions and their levels is important in determining your own emotional level and that of others. The scale is a tool that can be used in any profession that deals with people. In fact, the tone scale can be used in groups by applying the same emotional tones to the group. You will get the same feel of the group as you would with an individual person. Actors could use this scale to practice their reflection of emotions, but this is only for reference to demonstrate how powerful this scale is. It gives you the representation of all the emotional tones that need to be known to survive.

We know that we can change state at any given moment, which is very important, but most important are our consistent emotional tones. These are the tones that affect our life and must be the ones we focus on, but this does not mean we ignore emotions that we experience at any given moment; in fact, if we are to change our chronic tones, we must be able to change state at will. We must know our chronic emotional tones if we want them to work for us. We can do this by simply using the physiological and psychological techniques discussed earlier and applying them on a regular basis. Eventually the tone level we are experiencing most often is the tone level that becomes chronic and is achieved literally by changing the chemical composition within our body.

Our feelings are a representation of what chemicals are most present in our body. For example, if we are in a constant state of anger or fear, our body will chronically produce higher levels of adrenaline. If we are consistently in a state of serenity, then the chemical that is most present are endorphins. This is important to know, because if you are depressed and you want to use the GPA Life Cycle to improve your emotional tones, your chronic level will take some time to change. Eventually the chemical ratio within your body will reflect those emotions that you are consistently producing, and if this is the emotion of serenity, then your body will chronically have higher levels of endorphins. In short, you can change your chronic tone level with consistency. The more you purposefully change a tone to that of a higher tone, the more likely the higher tone will eventually become the most consistent tone. You are literally changing the set point of your emotional tone levels.

You can find your median by simply graphing your emotions throughout the day using the tone scale for a period of one week and then averaging the numbers to get the week's average. If you want to get much closer to your true average, do this for one month. It should be noted that one can experience a large swing on the emotional tone scale throughout any given day. For those who experience a larger swing or a very consistently low tone on a regular basis, an underlying emotional problem may exist. We will discuss this further in just a bit. Where there is trouble is when a person's emotional tones are low on a regular basis. This is diagnosed as manic-depressive, or depression, and can be extremely unhealthy both psychologically and physically. In fact, it can be the cause of many illnesses, so it is wise to address the issues as soon as possible. For those who experience a wide range of emotions, getting the average may be difficult, but one can assume that the individual's emotional control has been completely lost. This is most likely because of the control of past events and the triggers that have been created. This should not happen once you go through the release process, since all triggers and their control should be removed.

Once you take control back, you will have an easier time evaluating your average emotional tone.

A key factor in raising one's emotional tone is the concept of anticipation. We have all experienced looking forward to an event that has great meaning to us. An example is a drug addict, who may experience despair or hopelessness when they are without their fix, but as soon as he or she knows the fix is even on its way, you see their emotional tone rise dramatically. Even if the person is experiencing withdrawal symptoms, you will notice that the symptoms will dissipate when the addict is anticipating a fix that is on its way. Anticipation is extremely powerful; in and of itself, it can remove--or at minimum, reduce--the psychological and physiological symptoms of withdrawal.

Anticipation is often more exciting than the actual event. For this reason, people who are down or depressed are usually in a state of having no anticipation. In other words, when we have something to look forward to, we are generally more enthusiastic about life. When we set goals for ourselves, we are setting up something to look forward to, and if we have something to look forward to, we often experience greater joy in life. In fact, it is in the anticipation that we most often find our greatest fulfillment. I heard a statistic one time that said on average we only attain 8 percent of the goals we set. Another statistic I heard was even more disheartening. It states that 97 percent of those who set New Year's resolutions fail to attain them. This means that only 3 percent of these people accomplish their desire.

Something that is extremely interesting and supports the power of anticipation has to do with setting goals. We already know that a very low percentage of goals people set are ever attained. Why is this? I believe there are several reasons, one of which relates to emotions. When a person sets a goal, for example, to attain a million dollars, they believe the money is what they are after. The truth is that the money is only secondary. However, what they are truly after is the emotional state they get not only when they attain a million dollars, but also in the process of thinking about the reaching that goal. This supports the idea that anticipation is often a key motivating factor. It also makes sense, because if we were happy only when we attained a goal, we would certainly be unhappy much of the time. Think about any goal you have set and try to remember what gave you the most excitement--the anticipation or the goal itself. You will find that most of the time the anticipation is just as exciting.

Think about when you were a child and your parents told you were going to a special event, like the fair. Wasn't the anticipation part of the fun? Another example is Christmas, Hanukah, or your birthday. When you were a child, weren't you truly very excited in the days leading up to that special day? At times the event that we are waiting for, or the attainment of a goal, is disappointing. One reason this happens is because of the loss of anticipation. You are no longer looking forward to that outcome. With this in mind, we can certainly see that having goals and things to look forward to are extremely important to our emotional tones.

We also see people who experience midlife crises and begin to act out in uncharacteristic ways. Sometimes these actions are positive, and the only people suffering are those who are labeling that person as having a midlife crisis, or the individual himself, since his acts are being misinterpreted. Other times the crisis is a true crisis where the individual is in despair, because they see no hope for their future. In other words, their feeling is that it is too late to make up for the past. A person may see their job as a dead end, so there is no anticipation for the future and they thus experience depression. At other times we may experience a midlife crisis where we realize that what we expected never really came to be, but probably the real reason is because although we attained the level of success we were after, we have come to find that it was not what it was cracked up to be and we no longer have anything to look forward to or anticipate. Whatever the problem, it is important to know that in order to feel enthusiasm, one needs to have anticipation for some future event or outcome. This is why goals are so important--one can see the future with anticipation, but the goals must mean something and they must be realistic as well.

How does this help us in raising our tone? When life is good or when we are experiencing higher levels of emotional tone, it is because we are anticipating a bright future. When our future looks bleak, we often experience despair or depression. Have you ever noticed that when you were in a slump, you had no future aspirations, or the aspirations you had were lost? How about when you came out of the slump and life seemed much more exciting? It was when you could see a future that was appealing to you, and you began to experience anticipation for the attainment of the future. You also looked forward to the work that is required to attain the future that you are anticipating, because it is motivated by that anticipation. This is a drive, and no matter what needs to be accomplished, it will be done with purpose, because the anticipation fuels our actions.

As we get older, our dreams start to dwindle and we may feel like we're in a rut. This is because we are pretty much where we are, and the future is not looking much different or does not look like it can bring the level of meaning it once did. Once you get hold of a dream, you rise up the scale, and it is in the dream and the work toward attaining that dream that we find ourselves fulfilled. It is not the attainment of the dream that's so important, but it is in the anticipation and the work toward the dream that we find happiness. Look at rock stars, for example. Many go into the future never resurfacing in their fame, and many are diagnosed with depression or end up being addicted to drugs, or even dead. This happens because they hit a certain level of success and there is no way but down, or maybe they realize their dream is coming to an end and they can't see the future with anticipation. They have some pretty big shoes to fill, and it is very difficult to fill them if you don't have something to look forward to. Anticipation is a gem. It is a fuel that ignites our desires and the driving force that propels us to attain any desire we want. More important, it is the piece of the puzzle that gives us meaning and purpose to work day in and day out.

Think of it this way--if you won the lottery, would that experience be more fulfilling than earning the same amount of money by using your creative powers and the action to make your idea come to life? The answer is obvious; we all want to feel proud of our accomplishments, because this is the true reward--the ability to be productive and survive. It can be said that our true happiness comes from the work and not the attainment of the desire. This it not to say that winning the lottery wouldn't make you happy; it just wouldn't make you as fulfilled as accomplishments you achieve on your own. What makes you fulfilled and truly serene is your knowing that you are contributing toward a meaningful goal that brings joy and a sense of accomplishment. This is why we need to set small goals in the process of attaining a large goal. The small goals act as teasers--they're the carrot to keep us moving to the desired outcome. It is the ultimate pleasure that we are after, and in chasing that ultimate pleasure we are willing to experience great levels of pain--like long hours of tedious work, for example. In short, try to establish a clear vision of the future you want, and even if you never attain that exact future, you will likely be fulfilled as long as you work toward the attainment of that future and the desired outcome has a chance of being achieved.

The end result is important and is part of the process. If we knew there was no chance to attain the goals we set, we would never work to attain those goals. When we set goals, we set goals that others have attained or that we are fairly certain we have the ability to attain, and this gives us the anticipation required to move on. If a goal we set is not challenging enough, research shows we will not work toward its attainment. Research also shows that we won't attempt a goal we've set if it seems too much of a challenge. In both cases the anticipation is affected negatively. If the challenge is not difficult enough, then the rewards are not big enough to look forward to. If the challenge is too great, fear takes over and smothers anticipation. This means that when we set goals we need to make sure they are realistic. We also want to make sure they are goals we truly want. In the GPA

Goal-Setting technology, I have developed a process that takes into account many factors that will guarantee the attainment of the goals you set and the positive emotional tones that follow.

This may be a lot to absorb, but once you fully understand it, you will be well on your way to true happiness and fulfillment. Use this technology and you will find yourself living a more serene and fulfilling life. You will also affect your destiny; therefore you will be able to gain greater control of your outcomes. Finally, you will also have an affect on your environment and everything in it. In other words, you will not only be in control of you and your outcomes, but you will also be in control of your surrounding environment. All in all, you will be in control; therefore you will live the life you want to live, not the life someone else wants you to live. Take control of your life by taking control of your emotions, and I promise you will live a fulfilling life that can contribute to the wellness of the world.

CHAPTER 7

THE SOCIAL PILLAR

The Social Pillar is where we find our ability to develop relationships with others and ourselves. This is important since we are social creatures and since in order to be happy and effective, we must have the ability to develop working relationships that are consistent and lasting. Most people want to be around others who are respectful and trusting. We also want to be around people we can help, as you will see in the Pillar of Service. There are several characteristics that allow this to happen, but the greatest characteristic one can attain is that of integrity. This not only includes integrity with others, but more important integrity with ourselves. The relationship we have with ourselves is probably the most important relationship we will ever have; a respectful and trusting relationship with ourself is a prerequisite in developing relationships with others. For example, if we are dishonest with ourselves, how can we be honest with others? If we don't respect ourselves, how can we respect others? The important point here is that we must first attain trust and respect within ourselves if we are going to be respectful and trusting of others.

It is important we keep all promises to ourselves. Even the small promises we make to ourselves are damaging if we break them. In fact, we often lose our sense of worth because of the small lies we tell our self's every day. An example is when we say to ourselves that we are going to start eating healthy, then a week goes by and we haven't made any changes to our diet. Now, you may not even remember the promise, but your unconscious does, and when enough of these little broken promises build up, you will eventually get a sense of distrust with yourself that manifests itself as distrust to others. Your self-esteem and confidence are also lowered, because you did not honor a promise that you made to yourself. The point is to first build up trust and respect of yourself, and then you can start working on developing trust and respect with others.

Trust is earned, and it can be taken away in a second. You could be the most trusting, honest person on the planet, and if you fail one time in being honest, you will immediately attain the tag of being a dishonest person--not just dishonest in that particular event, but dishonest altogether. How do we build the trust we need to build quality relationships? The answer to this question is very simple: your actions must be consistent with your words. In other words, it is not so much what you believe as whether you back up your beliefs with actions that support those beliefs. You must also stay true to natural principles and laws. Honesty is a good example of a value one holds that is consistent with natural law, but in order for a person to be considered truly honest, he or she must always be honest. Honesty must be consistent for it to be effective, and when it is consistent and true, it can bring much joy to your life and the lives of those with whom you are in contact.

Whether we consider a person as an individual, as part of a small group, or as part of a large society, there are certain rules and laws set forth that the individual, group, or society must follow for their relationships to be effective. As individuals, we live by a set of rules we have internalized. As a group, we must live by the rules set by the group. For the good of our society as a whole, all members must maintain the integrity of the rules and laws that have been laid down. These rules or laws are called moral codes. In order to maintain group cohesion, it is imperative that all members, or at least the vast majority of members, agree with the moral codes and follow them. These moral codes are really a series of agreements that indicate what is right and wrong in terms of individual behavior, group behavior, and overall action. When an individual breaks a rule, the individual who broke the code is seen as lacking integrity. If this same person hides or otherwise lies about his or her immoral act, they are committing another transgression against the group, which causes even more animosity toward that individual who ignored the rule.

People often try to hide their transgressions in an attempt to avoid being found out or to avoid hurting the other person or persons against whom they committed the act. It is important to understand that even if your intention is to not hurt another person or persons, if you hide the transgression by lying, you are still committing another overt act against the individual or group. This cycle can create a web of lies that eventually tangles up the individual who is lying, and in the end they damage their reputation even more because by lying they have committed another act against the group. So if you make a mistake, do not hesitate to acknowledge and confess your mistake. Once you fess up, this overt act will lose its power over you and those around you. When you transgress against another, you are giving the transgression power to control your life, since the transgression leads to great turmoil and pain. You may recall that many of these painful events cause perception triggers that can direct your behavior without any command from you and take control of your life.

We must also consider the concept of ethics. Ethics are often cultural in nature, which can have problematic outcomes when dealing with people from other cultures. Understanding other cultures will allow us to be more sensitive, but it should be noted that some cultures hold values that we may never be able to accept. These people usually come from weak societies where intellectual progress is very low. They are ignorant to other ways and find themselves alienating themselves from the world. When this happens, they stop growing, and many problems occur that create greater problems in the future for all involved. If we are to continue our growth, it is important for us to understand the views of others and at minimum accept that they have a different set of beliefs. Many times you will end up taking on the ethics of another culture if it makes sense and works for you and your situation, but you do not have to agree with the other culture's beliefs. All you have to do is accept the fact that other people have a right to their beliefs as long as they do not go against natural law.

Values are another issue when it comes to culture, and again it is those societies or individuals who do not respect the values of others that stop progress altogether. Groups or individuals who understand that values are a personal choice are those who continue their growth and move forward. Again, we may take on the value of another if it works for us or for our situation, but we must make sure that doing so does not violate natural law.

It is important to discuss natural law if we are to really understand these concepts. We are given by nature rules that we must adhere to if we want to live with high survival potential. In other words, we must not violate laws that produce painful outcomes if we are to get along with others. These laws are ingrained in us; we know right from wrong in most cases, and we need to listen to our intuition if we are to respect these laws. Any time we violate a law, we run the risk of hurting ourselves and others in the process. If we adhere to the laws of nature, we will attain the pleasure and reward of doing so.

For example, if you want to get a work associate to do a task, you will not be able to do so if you violate that person in any way, or you will lower the likelihood of them helping you. On the other hand, if you adhere to the natural laws of relationships, such as the law of reciprocation, you will be more likely to get what you need. The law of reciprocation says if someone does something for you, you will have an urge to return the favor. These natural laws are a part of every aspect of life and can be found in any activity. The law of the harvest says we must plant the crop at a specific time, care for it as required, and remove it when it is ready. If you interfere with this law by planting late or not removing the crop at the right time, the crop will be ruined. If you apply this to relationships by understanding there are natural laws to follow, you will cultivate relationships that create a positive outcome for all parties.

If we violate the freedom of others by treating them as outcasts because of their values, we are casting ourselves out from the world. We need others to survive and they need us, but if we can't understand that we may sometimes have differences, we will never survive as a race. Accepting other people's values does not mean you are taking them on, it only says that you respect the other's freedom to live a life they desire, just as you want to live a life you desire. What would you do if a culture told you how to think, act, or behave? You would be lacking the freedom man deserves and to which he has a right.

If we want to experience fulfillment, we must hold a set of values that mean something to us and then act in ways that support those values. We must also hold a set of beliefs that empower us and then act on those beliefs. Many people have never deeply thought about what they value or what they believe. Such people react by taking on the values of a significant person in their life, like a parent, which unconsciously takes control of their behavior.

Our behavior is often a reflection of the values and beliefs we hold. If we go against these values and beliefs, we will find ourselves feeling guilty and out of touch. How many times have you felt like something was wrong, and you had a sense of guilt but you couldn't pinpoint why? One reason may be that we have been given values and beliefs that reflect the values and beliefs of another generation, which may be different than the values and beliefs of our own generation. When we act in ways that contradict either of these generations, we feel guilty. We may even get into a no-win situation, where no matter what we do, we are going against a value or belief we hold, and we get a sense of guilt that makes us shut down. This may even be the source of mental illnesses like depression.

When we actively look at our value system and consider the beliefs we hold, we are doing ourselves a huge service. By completing a values clarification and finding out what you believe in, you are giving yourself permission to do what you think is right, not what everyone else thinks is right. You are doing what humans were made to do--that is, to cognitively consider your values and make determination based on logic as to what you believe to be valuable.

With regard to beliefs, we get a similar result. We may hold a belief that was given to us by someone who had a bad experience--with money, for example. They may have tried to open a business and failed, because they did not do the proper research. They may believe that starting a business is a huge risk and that only those who are specially gifted could succeed. They may even say something like, "We are not genetically given the proper tools to be a financial success." This is an example of a limiting belief that is not true. It is a belief that will hold you back. You want to develop a set of beliefs that empower you. You could hold the belief that in order to be successful at owning a business, you must learn as much as you can and learn from the mistakes you make and other people make. This is an example of an empowering belief.

You can see how a limiting belief could hold you back and lead you to act--or should I say not act--in ways to bring you financial success. When you think deeply about your beliefs and ask yourself if they are limiting or empowering, you are allowing yourself to look for the beliefs that are controlling your destiny. When you remove those beliefs that hold you back, you open up a new avenue for success. When Colonel Sanders went out to sell his recipe for chicken, he held the belief that every "no" was another move to a "yes" and that it was only a matter of time before the "yes" would come. And eventually it did come. Imagine if he had held the belief that he could never become a success because he was too old. He was sixty-five when he went out to sell his recipe and became one of the most influential businessmen of our time.

The truth is if we believe we can't achieve something, we won't achieve it, because we will not give the required effort to win. On the other hand, if we believe we can achieve something, we will achieve it, because we will do what we believe we can do. The only reason we don't act is because we are afraid to fail. When we are not fearful, we will do whatever it takes to succeed. Hold beliefs that support your growth, and you are sure to be a great success.

How do we develop and cultivate relationships? How can we create trust and give others the ability to not fear our actions? The answer to these questions is also a direct result of what we value and believe and how we protect these values and beliefs. It is not so much what we believe or value as it is how we respect what we stand for. In other words, people most of the time value our relations not based on what we value or believe. They are more concerned with how you actually behave in light of your values and beliefs. If you say you value health and fitness and that you believe taking care of yourself physically will promote your health, but you are out of shape and you smoke, then your values and beliefs are not in line with how you represent yourself. This leads others to not trust you.

The same idea holds true within yourself. If you say you value learning and you believe learning is an important activity, but you never study, you are telling yourself that you cannot be trusted. In short, when our actions are in line with our values and beliefs, we build trust not only with others, but, more important, with ourselves. However, if your actions do not match your values and beliefs, you will eventually lose trust in yourself and others will question your intentions. This can lead to a number of problems, but the most obvious is the development of low self-esteem and the lack of strong relationships with others.

How do we create the integrity and trust needed for all relationships? The most powerful way is to create a code of conduct that reflects your values and beliefs. What is a code of conduct? A code of conduct is similar to a mission statement, but it is much more powerful. When you develop a mission statement, you are simply creating a statement about who you want to be. When you create it, you are only asked to write a statement that says this is how you want to be perceived. A code of conduct, however, is a reflection of the values you hold, the beliefs you hold and a statement that reflects your values and beliefs. The best way to create your code of conduct is after you have completed the values clarification exercises described earlier and after you have defined your empowering beliefs.

After you have defined your true values and have created a set of empowering beliefs, you can develop a code of conduct that maintains the integrity of your values and beliefs that you can live by. A code of conduct gives you a map to follow that will allow you to internalize your rules so they become a part of who you are. This is important because many times we are not consciously aware of what we value or what we believe. This can create times when we actually go against what we value or believe, which can leave us with the feeling that something is wrong. This can be seen when we feel guilt for no apparent reason. We have no clue as to the nature of the guilt, but it is there. The guilt is coming from an action we took that went against our true values or beliefs.

Many times our values and beliefs come from others who influence us, perhaps a parent or older sibling. We may have admired these people and taken their values and made them ours. This can be okay, but not if you don't really believe in those values. If they go against something that you value but have never really made you aware of the value, when you go against it, you feel a sense of guilt. The bottom line is this: whether your values come from you or from someone else, it is important to become aware of them. It is also important to organize them into a code of conduct so you can write them as a constitution, which gives them a more formal tone.

It is important for anyone who wants to develop their social aspect to understand the importance of having a well-defined set of values and beliefs. From these values and beliefs a code of conduct is created that gives a person the ability to function with integrity, therefore creating honesty and trust in their life.

Keeping an open mind with a critical thought process allows you to understand the values and beliefs of others and to develop your own set of values and beliefs. Our social skills depend on our ability to clearly define the values and beliefs from which we create the code of conduct we live by. In general, we respect others with different values and beliefs. Where problems arise, however, is when we say we value one thing but our actions are not in line with what we say we believe in or value. This causes us to distrust a person who is not acting in line with their values.

This also holds true within yourself; if your actions are not in line with what you value, the trust others have in you will be limited. If they know you follow a set of values and beliefs and you do something against their values and beliefs, they will generally accept you, as long as you are consistent with your own. It is important to note that if we hold values and beliefs that violate natural principle, we will never be accepted; in fact, we will lessen our survival potential, since we are acting against natural principles.

A real problem arises when we do not respect our own values and beliefs. This can happen unconsciously or consciously. When we go against what is important to us, we create the worst kind of distrust--distrust with ourselves. This is one reason we develop low self-esteem. We are literally lying to ourselves when we do something against what we value. For example, if I say I value health but I eat bad food throughout the day, then I'm lying to myself and showing others that I don't really care what I value. Another example is when we make a promise to ourselves and do not keep it. For example, if you were to say that you are going to quit smoking on New Year's Day, but like 97 percent of the population, you never fulfill the resolution, you are breaking a promise and literally saying to yourself that you are not important enough. This is one reason we should be careful never to make a promise that we are not certain we can keep. This holds true as well with others.

If you tell your kids, for example, that you are going to do something with them but fail to do it, it is a broken promise. The same is true if you promise yourself you are going to do something but fail to do so. You will be disappointed in yourself and begin to distrust yourself and your abilities, thus creating a low sense of self-esteem if the promise broken is to you, or a loss of trust from your kids if the promise was made to them. Both situations are bad, and both require deep consideration when deciding to make a promise. Try to make promises with care. If you make a promise and break it with yourself or someone else, it is much worse than if you just said no to the request.

How can we develop our ability to increase our social skills and create long-lasting relationships? We must develop our integrity and trust. To develop our integrity and trust, we must know what we value and what our belief systems are. It is important to note that our values and beliefs need to consider and respect natural principles, so when defining your values and beliefs you should consider natural principles carefully.

Natural principles are changeless, and if our values are in line with them, we find a solid foundation to work from. An example of this is the Constitution of the United States, which was based on the belief of freedom, which is a natural principle. No one wants to be enslaved, and for this reason we can say that freedom is a natural principle. With this in mind, we must have freedom as a value if we are to survive optimally. There are many natural principles, too many to cover here, but you will know in general whether your values and beliefs are congruent with natural principles. One way to make sure is to ask yourself if the value or belief you hold affects others in any negative way. If it does, it cannot be a value or belief that will work.

To begin, we must evaluate our current values and beliefs and ask ourselves if they are in line with natural principles. If they are not, get rid of them. If your values and beliefs are in line with natural principles, you should consider them. As mentioned above, we all value different aspects of life, and it is in our ability to maintain consistency with what we value that we build integrity and trust.

It's not so much the values that we hold that are important; rather, it is how well we reflect our values through our actions. We must remember that if our values or beliefs go against natural principles, we will lose integrity with others and even ourselves.

Many self-help programs ignore values and beliefs altogether, and if they do consider them, it is the author or creator telling us what to value and believe. You will not be able to hold another's values and beliefs with consistency, since they are not yours; therefore you will commit overt acts consistently and sever any or all relationships you have. This is just like getting them from your parents or someone you admire, as mentioned above, which can cause guilt that arises for no apparent reason. It is imperative that you define your own values and beliefs in order for them to be effective. When they come from you, you own them, and once they are internalized, your behavior becomes automatic and you will be able to develop the consistency required to develop trust.

The behavior that flows from our values and beliefs is what I call a code of conduct. In developing your code of conduct you must first develop your values and beliefs. To develop your values and beliefs, all that is required is a desire to ask yourself what you value, starting with those characteristics that make us who we are. These characteristics are the Pillars of Excellence: our spiritual, physical, mental, emotional, social, and service, and leadership aspects. Specifically, within each pillar, ask yourself, What do I value in   ? Fill in the blank with one of the characteristics listed above. For example, I may ask myself, What do I value physically? I will list all of the values I hold within the Physical Pillar. You will often find that your values can repeat themselves, so some of them can be combined. You should also do this with the roles you play. For example, if you are a husband, you may ask yourself, What do I value as a husband?

Next, it is important to define your beliefs, since these will play a major role in the development of your code of conduct. To define your beliefs you should understand what a belief is. A belief is a feeling or an emotion of certainty. In truth, your beliefs reflect whether or not you are meeting your values. As mentioned above, your beliefs either empower you or limit you. Beliefs are really rules we live by, so it is important to make sure they fit what is true for you.

Define the beliefs you have now, and ask yourself if they are limiting. Beliefs are limiting if they restrict us from doing what we really want to do or prevent us from experiencing life in any way. An example of a limiting belief is the person who says they are not smart enough to acquire great wealth. Here they have defined wealth as having to have a high IQ. From the Emotional Pillar we found that IQ was not the deciding factor in the area of hiring employees. Rather, EQ was more of a determinant, and if the individual had not limited his belief by thinking that being wealthy requires being smart, he could possibly have made more of an attempt to create great wealth.

Research has shown that people with higher EQs are more likely to experience greater wealth. This does not support a belief that says, "In order to be wealthy, I must have a high IQ." It makes me sick to think about all the dreams that have been left behind because somebody held a belief that limited their outcomes. My hope is that you will spend some time really defining your beliefs and determining whether they are limiting or empowering.

Another example can be in the definition of wealth. Most people believe wealth is simply a great deal of money, when wealth can actually be defined as a plethora of anything. If a person has a lot of friends, are they not wealthy? Define your beliefs so that they empower you. It's is amazing how many beliefs people have that they do not recognize as limiting. Beliefs can disguise themselves in many ways, so it is important to be a detective and try to find any reason a belief could limit you and then do something about it-- change a limiting belief to an empowering belief.

Once you know your values and beliefs, it is time to write your code of conduct. A code of conduct is the foundation of your actions and is where you find the direction of your decisions. It is important to note that your code of conduct is your way of maintaining congruency between your behaviors and your values and beliefs. Remember, your values and beliefs may change, and when this happens, consider your code of conduct and make any necessary changes. However, I do not suggest you change your values and beliefs too frequently, since this in itself may result in inconsistent behavior. Changing your values and beliefs must be done with care and consideration. In the beginning you may make quite a few changes, but over time, you will have modified and corrected any inconsistencies, so it will stabilize.

Writing your code of conduct does not have to be a dissertation; in fact, the shorter, the better in some cases. If you have to have a lengthy code, I would suggest that you create a short version as well that can be looked at and at least keeps your mind on what is important. Say as much as you can in very few words, and it only has to remind you of the values and beliefs you hold.

Once you have your code of conduct on paper, it is time to start internalizing it into your subconscious. To do this I have developed a process called the GPA Life Cycle, which will be covered in the GPA Life Enhancement technologies chapter in full. In short, the GPA Life Cycle guides you in reviewing your code of conduct, performing incantations that are in line with your pillars and roles, and visualizing the life you have just defined based on your pillars, values, beliefs, and your code of conduct. Doing this in a heightened emotional state helps to internalize your values and beliefs and allows them to connect to a great feeling. Doing this is like a drug. It will create a positive experience that moves you to want to focus on what is important to you. When you do this every day first thing in the morning, you are reminded of your values, beliefs, and your code, and if you stick with it for twenty-one days, it will become internalized and automatic.

Why twenty-one days? This is because our bodies change their chemical homeostasis in that period of time. This means that if we want to make an action consistent, we can do so by making that activity a part of our daily routine by connecting it to our psychology and our physiology using the GPA technology. I suggest that you continue doing the GPA Life Cycle for the rest of your life, because it gets you thinking daily about what is important to you and keeps you fresh on what you love. It also can create the opportunity to change anything you feel needs to change, because you are more familiar with what is important. You will be more apt to find congruencies in your values or your beliefs if you consistently maintain focus on them.

You will notice that your behavior will change to reflect your values and beliefs and that your code of conduct will begin to become a part of who you are. This will create your ability to act consistently and develop a trusting relationship with others and, more important, with yourself. Have fun with it and take your time--this is not work you need to rush. Develop the roots of your fruit by developing the behavioral platform from which you will launch your integrity. Again, there are some great performance-enhancement tools located in the GPA Life Enhancement technologies chapter that will help you in the process of getting your values and beliefs internalized. Remember the Emotional Pillar and how we use our psychology and physiology to enhance our emotions. When we combine these into all aspects of our lives, like our values and beliefs, we allow ourselves the ability to connect positive states to what is meaningful.

CHAPTER 8

THE SERVICE PILLAR

We all want to feel needed. The concept is evident in the gift of giving, where we can really find no selfless act. In other words, there is always something in it, not only for the receiver but for the giver as well. I know this sounds somewhat cynical, but this idea is ingrained in us so that we form healthy cultures and societies. Without the desire to give, societies would fail. However, it is important to understand that our giving can also cause the downward spiral of any society if the giving is done in ways that weaken the society. Today our giving has taken a turn toward the negative, and it is time to stop this downward trend if we want to see our society prosper.

In our need to feel needed, we tend to neglect how our gifts affect the receiver. Often the gifts we give hurt the person more than help them. Our welfare system is a perfect example, as it gives the individual no desire to grow; in fact, if the individual improves, the system is set up to make them think they are getting punished. For example, if they get a job, they are immediately cut off from the system, so why would they get a job? At minimum, why would they get a job that reports income? These people become a drain on society, and it's not their own fault. Our welfare system takes people out of the game of life in ways that prevent them from receiving any control of what happens to them. In short, the system affects some strong changes in aspects of motivational behavior that force people out of the game of life.

I experienced the pain of giving in the wrong way several times, or perhaps I should say the people I gave to experienced great pain because of how I contributed. I used to help one family at a time by giving them money, thinking it would get them back on their feet, or at least reduce the suffering they were experiencing. The problem was that although my intent was to help get them back in the game of life, my giving only served to put them on the couch and in front of the TV. I gave with the thought I was helping, when in fact I often made things worse. All the people I helped had jobs in the beginning, but most of them eventually quit their jobs, because I was giving them no reason to go to work. I foolishly thought they would pay off bills or put the money away in savings to get ahead, but most of the recipients eventually took too much advantage of the gift. They would quit their jobs, go out and buy things they didn't need, or waste the money on drugs or alcohol. I have to say that I too would want to quit the jobs they held, as they were not the most pleasant places to work, mostly factory work.

However, many of the recipients of my gifts started to expect the money, and in one case a person even threatened to kill my family and me. I had helped him receive an insurance claim whereby he received a significant amount of cash. Since I felt he no longer needed my help, I decided to take the money I was giving to him and give it to someone else who needed it. His reaction really bothered me, and quite frankly it led me to stop giving altogether for a while. Why did this happen?

In my desire to help--or should I say in my desire to feel needed--I gave to these families with no strings attached, so they had no incentive to grow. Once they knew they could get by without a job, they would quit their job. After several of these instances, I began to get suspicious of people in general and took on a few new beliefs that were a bit negative until I realized what I had done. They were actually doing what most people would do in the same circumstances.

Looking back at the situation, I have to admit that I would have been tempted to do the same things myself. They were taking the easy route, which is what most humans would do. In fact, it is built into us through our ability to reason. We are given the ability to find the path of least resistance. I needed to change this, however, because all I was doing was making these people dependent on me instead of themselves and leading them to drop out of the game of life. My giving did not motivate them at all; in fact, it created in them a lack of motivation. This resulted in their having no connection with life and actually started to lead to depression in some of them.

I knew I needed to change my approach in how I contributed to the world. I was at a loss, but I knew if I continued doing as I had been doing, I would cause more harm than good. I was really at a loss and had no idea what to do. As mentioned above, I almost gave up. I was even cynical about the situation until I realized through research that human behavior is often motivated by outside forces. In short, I realized that we often are moved in certain directions automatically, depending on the influence. Influence can come in many forms, which we will discuss in greater detail in the Leadership Pillar. For now I want to show you how influence is not just an aspect that comes from others. It can come from objects or material things just the same, and in some cases with greater force.

When we lack or are doing without something, we are very sensitive to material possessions. When we have abundance, however, material goods become less of a focus and we begin to seek emotional aspects. I decided to read and study everything I could on the subject of contribution. I also researched any topic that would relate to the concept of contribution, from its definition to how giving affects the internal forces of another person. What I found was simply eye-opening. Most important, I realized that gifts come in many different forms. I learned that the best gifts to give and to receive are those that promote a person's ability to live higher on the survival scale. I began to make note of different ways I could help the poor and asked myself what would best serve those who are living in poverty. Like most people, I believed that money would be best gift. In fact, our first idea is usually to give the very thing that someone lacks, but this is often the wrong thing to do.

I rarely give money anymore, but when I do, I now set a time limit so that the recipient is made aware of an end point and of my intention to help them either pay off their debt or get back on their feet with savings in the bank. I never cut them off before the time limit, even if they make more money on their own, because I believe they should be rewarded for their gains. Once the time is up, they know they are expected to continue to work, and they know they will receive no more money from me, so they are more apt to put away what they can. In fact, I make it clear that I expect them to follow a certain financial system that teaches them how to be responsible with money. If they do not follow the system, I simply inform them that since it appears they have enough of their own money, my help is no longer needed. I also have them sign a contract that states that if they do not follow the system, they will have to reimburse me. In the time allotted, I insist that they get off of welfare at some point, where they can begin to care for themselves. If they fail to do this, or if they reapply for welfare at any point, they must pay back any money I gave them. They have no choice, since it is in our contract.

Our welfare system needs to change and needs to change quickly. We are ruining lives because those on welfare have no desire to live and experience life with all of its usual ups and downs. If our welfare system limited the time one receives welfare, it would motivate people to improve their conditions. With the current system, however, they are being punished for working and highly rewarded for not getting a job. With a limited system that rewarded the person to find a job, the individual would be rewarded for becoming productive and punished for not being productive. I know there will always be a few people who take advantage of the system by never doing anything that might take their free money away, but this system would kick those people out and force them to work--and therefore to grow. In fact, it would be a much more generous gift then just paying them to lie around. Survival is a big motivator, so I would venture to say that those who are mentally fit would eventually realize that eating is more important than lying around watching reruns of Jerry Springer.

How should we give as individuals? This is a very tricky question, but it is easy to answer if you understand what giving should represent. Giving should never hurt another person, and it should look out for their welfare in terms of what is best for all parties. Laws are intended for the protection of you from me and vice versa. This says that a law should only protect you from others and not from yourself, unless of course you are mentally unfit. The same holds for giving--we should always give in ways that help others grow. With this in mind, we can say that money is not the only gift that can help. In fact, this idea puts giving money at the bottom of the list and places more important gifts at the top. What can we give besides money? We can give emotionally. Here we can empathize with another and try to understand their problem. We can also give love, by showing genuine care for another. This is one of the greatest gifts we can give, because often the receiver will end up loving back.

I want to make a point about giving and that is this. We are designed to give back at minimum that which we receive. We all know door-to-door salesmen who bring gifts or the Hare Krishnas who offer a flower before they ask for a donation. These techniques are very effective, and it is one of the reasons a law has been put on the books that says we have three days to rescind on our purchases. Giving to receive is very powerful, and for this reason it is said that you will ultimately receive more than you give. This works, and it works every time. Give and you will be showered with gifts. These gifts are not always money and often come in forms that we don't recognize as a gift. One gift that we often receive is the gift of giving. The person doing the giving is the one who ultimately receives the greatest gift, which is why I say all giving is selfish. In fact, try to think of a gift that is not selfish and you will see that giving is rarely for selfless reasons.

What else can we give? The most powerful gift, next to love, is the gift of knowledge. Knowledge can give someone the gift of life. It can give someone the gift of education so that they can produce. To give knowledge for the true sake of helping another person is one of the least selfish gifts we can give. However, when you give the gift of knowledge, you also receive the gift of furthering your own knowledge, because teaching someone a topic allows you to internalize it deeper. In fact, Jesus gave the gift of knowledge. It was his way, and this is what made him so great. Of course he gave his life, which is the least selfish gift one can give. Now you maybe saying, "All right, John, you're nuts if you think Jesus was selfish," but if you think about it, he was doing it to please God.

The end result for Jesus was to fulfill God's desires. Doing so would please God, and Jesus knew that pleasing God would also provide him with a seat at the right hand of God. Before we go any further, I want to make certain that although I am using Christianity as an example, I am not asking you to become a Christian. This is not the purpose of this work, and that is something you need to decide for yourself. I merely want to demonstrate that even in the most extreme cases of giving, there's always something in it for the giver. This doesn't mean that Jesus, or for that matter anyone else who gives, was only looking out for himself. Giving is in our nature for a reason. First, giving provides us with the ability to come together and stay together as a human race. It also provides pleasure for those who are giving, because it gives that person a great sense of meaning. Jesus was no different, and he found great pleasure in giving, even in giving his life.

One of the most powerful gifts that Jesus gave was knowledge; it was the gift of knowledge that made him so famous and well loved. We too can give knowledge, because we all have knowledge to give.

Knowledge is powerful, because it gives the receiver the tools to live life with greater success, which provides them with a higher survival potential.

Giving knowledge can have extraordinary effects on both parties. First the giving of knowledge helps the giver further understand the knowledge they are giving. It also gives the receiver the gift of being able to function at higher levels. Gaining knowledge, giving in general, also has positive effects on our physiology. When we give we feel good, because our bodies produce endorphins, which in turn creates a sense of euphoria. The chemical reactions involved are similar to the effects of heroin, but they are much stronger and of course have no bad side effects. Although giving can be somewhat addicting, this type of addiction is healthy, because it drives you to give even more and can be achieved without robbing, stealing, or killing. It is at our fingertips at all times, and it has a healthy effect on our body in that it lowers blood pressure and heart rate, just to name a couple of its physical benefits.

When we give the wrong gift we will eventually experience pain, because we will see the recipient of our gift enter a downward spiral. In the end, we too will fall from grace, because we will see the aftermath of our actions. I was depressed for months when I realized my gifts were for the wrong reason and had hurt the receiver tremendously. The point is that when we give, it must come from a spirit of true desire to help, and it must be a gift that helps the recipient in positive ways.

Giving someone the ability to be dependent on themselves is a gift of life and allows the person to be free. Imagine what it would feel like to take money from the state and become dependent on that money. This is a form of slavery, because the person's freedom is literally taken away. To truly give, we must help the person to become totally independent. I call it getting one off of welfare and onto self-care. When we give another person the will to live--the will to experience not only the pleasure life has to offer, but also the pain--we give them the greatest gift life can offer. The point is, when we experience only pleasure in life, like the welfare recipient who does not worry about income, we have no baseline on which to gauge pleasure and pain. In other words, how do we experience pleasure if pain does not exist? Pleasure can be defined as leaving a painful state, and if no pain exists, then how can we truly experience pleasure? I know this sounds philosophical, but it reminds us that our most fulfilling moments in life are our ability to overcome challenges. The greater the challenges we face, the more fulfilling the experience. With this we can understand that pain is a gift that precedes fulfillment.

Giving someone knowledge is a great way to help them improve their current condition. Next to love, knowledge is the most important gift with regard to giving another the ability to succeed. With this in mind, knowledge is the most important factor in living higher on the survival scale. Another gift can be that of health, whereby we teach another person how to live more healthy and develop a life of wellness. Still another gift is that of helping people to reach higher emotional states. We can do this by following the principles we talked about in the Emotional Pillar chapter. Of course the gift of friendship is a gift we give to someone who has earned our trust, and we have earned theirs as well. Finally, the gift of empowerment--that is, leadership via influence--is a key factor in moving another person into higher levels of living.

With all of this in mind, you could go and find a person who is jailed by welfare or another dependency, teach them the Pillars of Excellence, and literally coach them into living again. In fact, I offer a coaching certification program that will give you the ability to bring this knowledge to others and in turn help the world in significant ways. Of course the people you help, if they follow the program, will also help others help themselves, and this can result in a snowball effect where more and more people are being helped.

You don't have to give what you don't have; you are giving somebody something you do already have. We don't have to give money or material possessions to contribute in positive ways. The truth is that the gift of material items, such as money, is one of the least effective gifts in terms of helping another person. Many people fail to give because they lack abundance, but with giving knowledge you do not deplete the gift as you would with money. You actually increase that gift inside of you. This shows us that giving allows us to receive. The Bible talks of getting back when you give, and this is what I am talking about. When you give, you open the door to receive and you inspire others to want to give back. This is seen in the law of reciprocation, where we feel obligated to return something when we receive from others. For example, advertisers today often give us something before they ask us to purchase their item. They do this because you are more likely to by their product after you have received something from them.

This is true with the Hare Krishnas, who may provide you with a flower before asking for a donation. Research shows that a return of 93 percent is realized when a gift is provided before a request. In other words, if someone gives you something and then asks something of you, you are more likely to fulfill their need than if they had not given you a gift at all. This is a natural principle in human relations, so put it to use and give as much as you can. Open your eyes to those in need, and give with all your heart. It works! When you give to others, they will feel obligated to give back to you, often giving more than what they received. However, keep in mind that there are some people who are not affected by the law of reciprocation. These are usually the antisocial, whose only concern is with themselves. These people don't want help; they want life given to them with no strings attached.

This brings me to an important point: don't waste your time helping another person who is not willing to help themselves. When you refuse to help another person because they are unwilling to help themselves, you're actually helping them more than if you were to just give them money. Often a person needs to hit rock bottom before they realize things must change. It would be greedy if you helped them by giving them money, because all you would be after is an easy way to make yourself feel good. The point is that for someone to improve, they must want to receive the gift you bear.

We can help others by being an example and living a life that is consistent with growth and productivity, and eventually we may rub off. We must be responsible in how we give, and we must maintain our value of human life. Everyone deserves to live life, and if we take this life away from someone, as we do with welfare, we are literally taking their life from them so that we can get the good feeling we want when we give. This is selfish, and we need to examine all gifts we give.

Another important point is that we must also be very careful not to allow another to give to us any gift that may make our own life less productive or worse off. This can be tough, but if you are faced with the receipt of money, for example, that could help another person more and you accept it, you are only hurting yourself. If you are taking money from a source and you see that you are losing vitality, get rid of it no matter how good it feels, because eventually it will lead to pain. Give to others with the intent to do well, receive from others only with the intent to grow and live a more productive life, and you will experience a great life. Don't jail anyone or let anyone jail you by allowing the gift to control you or another person.

CHAPTER 9

THE LEADERSHIP PILLAR

We always want to find that perfect way to perform our work. Many times we want the one perfect way, and this is simply not going to happen. We must learn to accept that situations require different approaches, and this is no different for leadership effectiveness. To be an effective leader, you must be able to read the situation and apply the right leadership style.

There are two types of leadership and several styles of leadership to be considered. With regard to types, we can break it down to personal leadership and leadership of others. Personal leadership is your ability to effectively lead your own life, and this must be done before you can effectively lead others. We have all experienced the leader who says by way of action, "Do as I say, not as I do." This is very ineffective and such leaders fail every time. Those who practice what they preach are the ones who can influence others and succeed as leaders. Leadership of others can only happen if you are an effective leader of your own life.

The Pillars of Excellence program is really a self-leadership program in that you are guided to develop your life based on the characteristics that make you who you are. To lead your self it is imperative that you cultivate each area and know exactly where you are now and where you are going in each area of life. This requires a great deal of creative thought and imagination where you actually see yourself in the future where you want to be. It also requires you to be a diligent planner, saying yes to activity that takes you toward your future desires and no to those activities that take you away from your future desires. The Pillars of Excellence program uses the GPA Life Management system, which was created so you could set your goals, define the purpose of your goals, and create the action plan in attaining your goals. The GPA Life Management system is developed using the GPA Goal-Setting technology, which guides you in setting and achieving any goal you desire. The approach uses specific techniques that motivate you in attaining the goals. We will touch on it here so that you can use the data in your current planner, but you can also order the GPA Life Management system and the GPA Goal-Setting technology from the Pillars of Excellence through our Web site at: www.pillarsofexcellence.com, or you can call us at (513)770-0102. We also offer coaching to guide you in developing the life of your dreams using all the Pillars of Excellence technologies for the greatest benefit.

The system is simple and very effective. First, you want to set your goals for each pillar and each role you play. Once you have set your goals, you want to define the purpose for attaining your goals. This is where most people fail in goal attainment. The goals most people set are the goals of others. For example, if you set a goal to quit smoking, it will not happen unless it is your desire to quit. Most people first try to quit because someone has asked them to. You have got to want it yourself. Once you have set the goals you want and have defined the purpose of attaining the goals, you must develop the actions you must take to attain your goals. Having a strong enough purpose will be enough to get you to take consistent action. Most goal-setting programs tell you to set goals and then immediately start taking action. The problem with this is that you will only take action in the beginning, because the initial purpose was never decided on, and your motivation will fade away.

Now that you have the goals, purposes, and actions, all that is needed is for you to put it in your planner. When you plan you should plan a month in advance. This gives you the ability to step into the future and see the results, which will motivate you even further. If you are using the Pillars of Excellence planner, it will guide you in doing the required steps from beginning to end. If you are using a different planner, that is okay, because the system will work with any planner--you just have to tailor the planner to fit the GPA Life Management system.

Once you have set the goals in the planner, you can define the purpose for attaining the goals. Make the purpose strong and include as much detail as possible in your definition of the purpose. Once you have defined the purpose, you can set the action plan in the planner for a month in advance. This again allows you to see the end results. I would suggest that you break your action into steps so that you will hit mini-goals along the way. This will give you little wins and therefore get you motivated to continue, because you are seeing results.

To effectively lead your own life, you must know where you are, where you are going, why you are going there, and how you will get there. The Pillars of Excellence program guides you in doing this and will provide you with an organized way to attain any goal you want.

To begin our discussion on leading others, I would like to define leadership, and from there we can look into the styles of leadership that can be used to be effective. I would also like to cover the current beliefs about leadership style and the effects it can have on your success as a leader.

With regard to the definition of leadership, many definitions exist; in fact, there are probably as many definitions of the word "leadership" as there are numbers of people who have attempted to define it as a concept. This can get awfully confusing for anyone trying to develop their leadership skills. Some of these definitions include: the behavior of a person directing the activities of a group toward a shared goal (Hempill and Coons 1957, 7). Leadership is also defined as "the influential increment over and above mechanical compliance with the routine directives of the organization" (D. Katz and Kahn 1978, 528). Another definition of leadership is "the process of making sense of what people are doing together so that people will understand and be committed" (Drath and Palus 1994, 4). Still another definition is "the ability of an individual to influence, motivate, and enable others to contribute toward the effectiveness and success of the organization" (House et al. 1999, 184). The above definitions sound good, and all of them hold some truth. However, they all lack the definition of leadership's full meaning with regard to its application. Most of the above definitions focus on leadership of others, but fail to mention the most important aspect of leadership--leadership of self. I point this out before we move on to leading others, because I want to emphasize how important it is to effectively lead yourself before you can lead others.

We all want the perfect program in anything we do, and this is no different in leadership. I'm often asked to define the perfect program, the one approach that is the best, and I always answer the question by saying that the best program depends on the situation. In other words, if you want to be an effective leader, you must lead according to the situation. You must be able to recognize what style of leadership will fit the given situation. There is no one best approach except the one that uses the best style for the situation. For this reason I want to discuss some of the most common styles of leadership that are in use today, and you can then learn to decide which is best for the situation at hand. At first it may be difficult to determine the right style, but eventually you will become good at evaluating the situation and then choosing the right approach. Practice makes perfect, so all I can tell you is practice, practice, practice.

I would first like to touch on aspects of effective leadership and cognitive resource theory that are important--specifically, a look into the contingency, charismatic, and transformational leadership theories.

It first should be noted that although many theories of leadership exist, research has proven to be somewhat inconclusive on which theory is most effective (Robbins 2003). Leadership effectiveness has been connected to certain traits the leader possesses, which include intelligence, drive, and self-confidence (Robbins 2003). These traits alone cannot constitute effective leadership. Behavior of a leader has been shown to provide both positive and negative results.

Leadership studies made at Ohio State University had the purpose of identifying leadership behavior and developing questionnaires that described this behavior (Yukl 2002). After factor analysis, two leader behavior categories surfaced, one of which dealt with task objectives and the other with interpersonal relations. Consideration was given to interpersonal relations where the leader is friendly, supportive, and looks out for the general welfare of subordinates. The task objective, or initiating structure, concerned itself more with tasks like defining roles and goals. These two categories were found to be independent.

Research showed mixed reviews of these two behavior categories. In some of the studies where a leader was task- or objective–oriented, subordinates performed better than those under a leader using interpersonal relation skills. In other studies, the opposite was revealed. The only consistency showed more satisfaction among subordinates of a leader who was concerned with interpersonal relationships (Yukl 2002).

Similar studies in Michigan revealed three types of behaviors that differentiated between effective and ineffective managers. They are:

1. Task-oriented Behavior. This theory states that an effective manager focuses on planning and scheduling work, coordinating activities, and providing support and assistance when needed.

2. Relations-oriented Behavior. This theory says the manager would not put task-oriented behavior in front of human relations. The manager was friendlier, considerate, and revealed trust and confidence in the subordinate, which helped them advance their careers. In relations-oriented behavior, the leader is not only interested in completing a task, they are also interested in the people involved.

3. Participative Leadership. These leaders were more group oriented. They promoted cooperation and offered to resolve conflict. This type of leader guides the group in resolving a task (Yukl 2002).

The 1960s gave birth to a concept called "High-High Leader." This theory states that there is a balance where effective managers are not only concerned with production but are also concerned with people. In this case, a high-high leader is goal oriented and encourages the setting of realistic goals that will improve product quality (Yukl 2002).

Another important aspect of effective leadership concerns itself with communicating clear objectives without micromanaging. If too much direction is prescribed, resentment can be expected (Yukl 2002). Effective communication affords the leader the opportunity to develop trusting relationships that are of great importance to leadership effectiveness. If a manager wants to lead effectively, he must develop trust among his subordinates (Robbins 2003). Ways to do this include treating others fairly, being open and honest, being consistent, keeping promises, developing competence, and maintaining confidence (Robbins 2003).

An effective leader also provides recognition in the form of praise, appreciation, and rewards. Rewards not only help to motivate individual behavior, but also have influence on others when the reward is made public (Robbins 2003). Leaders today are also faced with diversity. The leader's behavior toward people from other cultures can have significant consequences. The leader is also faced with cross-generational factors--workers who grew up influenced by the Great Depression, the boomers of the 1960s, the Gen-Exers, and the Nexters--all of whom are influenced and hold different values and ideas that generate happiness (Robbins 2003; Aamodt 2004). In this scenario, the leader of today has to be both a psychologist who can understand and predict individual behavior, and a sociologist who must understand culture (Aamodt 2004).

Having discussed effective leadership, we must now find the view of leadership that can best foster effectiveness. Three factors must be defined. They are participative leadership, delegation, and empowerment (Robbins 2003; Yukl 2002). Participative leadership states that a leader allows subordinates, and other sources outside of an organization, to have influence on the decision-making process (Yukl 2002). Delegation involves the assignment of responsibilities and authority to a subordinate. Empowerment can be viewed as assigning responsibility to a person to create positive development of that person's self-worth (Ronit et al. 2003). With regard to empowerment, a leader can also use this to develop a person's capacity to function at higher levels (Ronit et al. 2003), which, as mentioned above, develops self-confidence in both the subordinate and the leader in terms of confidence in the subordinate (Yukl 2002). Empowerment must be handled with care and given to the right people. If empowerment or delegation is given to the wrong people, unsatisfactory work could result; in turn, confidence can be crushed (Yukl 2002; Ronit et al. 2003).

It is obvious that delegation and empowerment are closely connected to participative leadership; in fact, participative leadership could not exist without delegation and empowerment. It should be noted that with regard to delegation, a leader does not just dump, but delegates for the right purpose (Covey 2003). An example of dumping would be for the leader to eliminate unwanted tasks simply because the tasks are not enjoyable.

For a leader to be effective, she must be able to determine the best possible course of action to be taken in the search for the solution of any problem (Gordon 1977). To do this, a leader must depend on others, which participative leadership allows. A leader cannot know everything and at times must seek outside help from either within the organization, from consultants, and/or from another organization all together (Gordon 1977). Participative leadership allows the leader to delegate the decision or a task to another if the other person is better equipped to solve the problem and/or if the other person allows for the leader to focus on other tasks (Thompson, Aranda, Robbins 2000).

Cognitive resource theory looks at the cognitive ability of leaders (Yukl 2002). It looks at intelligence and experience as they relate to group performance (Yukl 2002). The theory talks of interpersonal stress that is present in a leader and says that stress is the trigger for the use of intelligence or experience. If a leader is under low stress, the theory says, his abilities are more directed by intelligence than they are by experience. If a leader is under high stress, the theory states, his ability is more closely tied to experience than it is to intelligence (Yukl 2002).

It is important to note that some jobs differ in regard to what is defined as high-level stress (Yukl 2002). For example, a CEO of a company might be under high levels of stress because the competitive environment has caused a great deal of profit loss. This high level of stress, though it does affect performance, cannot be similar in nature to the high level of stress, for example, that a pilot experiences in a potential life-threatening situation, like catastrophic engine failure.

Another factor that should be considered within the cognitive resource theory is in regard to stress tolerance. There is no doubt that both a CEO and a pilot react to stress in similar ways, but one must consider the stress tolerance of the individual. People handle stress differently (Weiten 2002; Selye 1984); there are those who can handle a great deal of stress and function at normal levels, while others flip out at the first indication of a problem.

The next issue involves experience. The cognitive resource theory states that experience will affect a leader's performance in high-stress situations (Yukl 2002). Experience can be measured in several ways. One way is to measure experience in terms of years of service. A more precise measurement should look at experience in terms of task experience (Yukl 2002).

Research in cognitive resource theory has had its limitations. Most studies performed looked at Fiedler's LPC (least preferred coworker) contingency model, explained below, and then applied it to the cognitive resource theory. This does not give the cognitive resource theory the complete test (Yukl 2002). It would be beneficial to compare outcomes with combinations of intelligence and experience and relate them to high- and low-stress situations (Yukl 2002). Another problem that research has neglected is related to experience. Research should focus more on task experience and not so much on position experience (Yukl 2002). Current research has also neglected human relationship factors. A more experienced leader has had more time in developing relationships that can support them under stress, and this should be considered when performing future research (Yukl 2002).

There is no doubt that stress affects decision quality (Thompson, Aranda, Robbins 2003). It is obvious that experience can help a leader function at higher levels, but one aspect that has been ignored is helping the leader deal more effectively with stress.

Because the prediction of leadership success is complex, the contingency theory tries to put focus on situational influences (Robbins 2003). Five main contingency theories exist: path-goal, leader substitutes, multiple-linkage, Fiedler's LPC Contingencies, and cognitive resource (Yukl 2002). Of these five, three receive more attention: the Fiedler leadership model, path-goal, and leader participation (Robbins 2003).

The Fiedler model looks at how situations moderate leadership effectiveness and the least preferred coworker, LPC scores (Yukl 2002). Fiedler believed that a leader's style is the key to leadership success (Robbins 2003). He created a questionnaire that contained sixteen contrasting adjectives to determine whether a person is task oriented or relationship oriented (Robbins 2003). Fiedler wanted to know how a respondent would describe a person they least enjoyed working with (Robbins 2003; Yukl 2002)). He believed that a response about another person reveals more about the respondent than it does about the person in question (Robbins 2003; Yukl 2002). If a respondent talked in positive terms of the least favored person they worked with, then Fiedler believed the respondent had high regard for personal relations and would label him or her "relationship-oriented" (Robbins 2003; Yukl 2002). If the respondent talked in unfavorable terms of the other person, Fiedler believed the respondent was more productive conscious and labeled him or her "task-oriented" (Robbins 2003; Yukl 2002).

Once Fiedler assessed leadership style via the LPC questionnaire, he would then match that leader with one of three situational factors. They are leader-member relations, task structure, and position power (Robbins 2003; Yukl 2002). Leader-member relations describe the confidence, trust, and respect a leader has with his or her subordinates. Task-structure describes whether job assignments given to a subordinate are structured or unstructured (Robbins 2003; Yukl 2002). Position power reflects the influence a leader possesses and his or her ability to implement action--that is, hiring, firing, discipline, and so forth (Robbins 2003). Fiedler's model would then look at a situation in regard to three contingency variables. A leader could have good or poor leader-member relations, high or low task structure, and strong or weak position power (Robbins 2003).

The path-goal theory says it's the leader's responsibility to support and assist subordinates in achieving their goals through direction and ensuring the subordinates goals are in line with the objectives of the group or organization (Robbins 2003). For the leader to be effective, it is important that the subordinate accepts the leader's behavior, which will happen if the subordinate views the leader as one who satisfies a subordinate's immediate and/or future need (Robbins 2003; Kirkpatrick and Locke 1996).

The leader participation model was developed by Victor Vroom and Phillip Yetton. This model was developed to recognize leadership behavior and participation in decision making (Robbins 2003). It is believed that a leader's behavior should adjust according to task structure (Robbins 2003). The model provided a set of rules that could be followed to tell the user how much participation should be used in varying situations (Robbins 2003). The model contains seven contingencies and five alternative leadership styles (Robbins 2003). A new model has been developed that expands the number of contingency variables from seven to twelve.

Research has shown that low levels of performance may be a result of a poor match between the organization and a task (Hollenbeck et al. 2002). The current approaches used in applied psychology with regard to contingency theory look at how a person fits within an organization (Hollenbeck et al. 2002). It is believed that benefit could be realized if fit-based approaches would expand in other directions (Hollenbeck et al. 2002). In regard to organizational theorists, they focus more on external fit in relation to a group or organization and task environments (Hollenbeck et al. 2002). Value could also be realized if research looked at both internal and external fit (Hollenbeck et al. 2002).

I would now like to define charismatic leadership. Transactional leaders guide or motivate subordinates through direction and clarification of role and task requirements (Robbins 2003; Kirkpatrick and Locke 1996). Transformational leaders, also known as charismatic leaders, motivate subordinates to develop their own self-interests that reflect concern for the organization (Robbins 2003; Kirkpatrick and Locke 1996). Five attributes can separate a charismatic leader from a noncharismatic leader. They are as follows:

1. Charismatic leaders are confident in their ability.
2. They have vision that creates a better future.
3. They are committed to the goal.

4. They behave in ways that are perceived as novel, unconventional, and counter to norms.
5. They are looked at as shakers and not caretakers of the status quo (Robbins 2003).

Research has shown that subordinates working under a charismatic leader are more self-assured, perceive meaning to their work, show more support for the leader, are willing to work longer, and generally perform higher than those working under a noncharismatic leader, even if that leader is effective (Robbins 2003; Kirkpatrick and Locke 1996).

Three core components have been identified in the area of charismatic leadership with regard to performance and attitudes. They are vision, vision implementation through task quos, and communication style (Kirkpatrick and Locke 1996). An effective vision arouses followers' needs and values, departs from status quo but remains accepted, and leads others toward goals and away from undesirable performance (Kirkpatrick and Locke 1996).

Since the terms "transformational" and "charismatic" leadership are often used interchangeably (Kark et al. 2002), I would like to provide a distinction between the two. In charismatic form, a leader provides vision and offers solutions in extraordinary situations (Yukl 2002). The charismatic leader attracts followers by instilling belief in a vision (Yukl 2002). Transformational leadership, on the other hand, connects with the subordinate in terms of moral values and ethical issues and motivates subordinates by being concerned with a subordinate's self-interest (Yukl 2002; Ronit et al. 2003). The values are relevant in the relationship and include honesty, fairness, responsibility, and reciprocity (Yukl 2002).

In conclusion, it must be noted that effective leadership is dependent on the situation. An effective leader recognizes the situation and applies the best approach. At times a combination of theories is best, at other times one style may be sufficient. The effective leader must know what combination will be most effective.

Effective leadership is really influence, where one person is trying to excite another about the fulfillment of a certain task in which the completion of the task respects quality. If we can get others to really care about the project at hand, then we can get others to carry out that project with great success. However, if the individual is not excited about the task, they will never produce the quality of work needed for optimum success. In order for anyone to be excited about a task, they must first get excited about their own lives. For this reason, it is very important to pick for your team a group of people who are good self-leaders and who have their lives in order. Once you select the right people, all that is needed is the ability to influence, which is a very effective tool in getting others to do what you need them to do. I will give you six specific laws about influence that you can learn and use for great success.

Influence is the key component, and this is what must be understood if you ever want to lead anyone, including yourself. Remember that leadership is nothing but influencing others to complete a task. To do this you must understand the power of influence. There are six specific laws we will cover in regard to influence, which I call the six laws of leadership. They include:

1.   the law of reciprocation
2.   the law of commitment and consistency
3.   the law of social proof
4.   the law of liking
5.   the law of authority
6.   the law of scarcity

When you know these laws and understand them to the point of being able to use them, you will be able to use the leadership style I call influential leadership. This style of leadership works off the principles of human behavior and is directly connected to the laws of influence. They work and they are proven to work. This is the most effective leadership style you will ever use. Learn it, know it, and use it.

Leadership is really the ability to influence yourself or others to complete a task. When we want someone to do something, or we want ourselves to do something, we are simply influencing ourselves or others to complete the task. Influence, then, is a major tool in leadership, and it must be thoroughly understood. People operate under some pretty strict rules, natural rules that motivate them to behave in certain ways, and a good leader should be able to use these internal laws that exist in each and every one of us if they want to be effective.

There is an internal law within each of us that says we should try to repay, in kind, what another person has provided us. This is the law of reciprocation, where one is given something and the person receiving feels the desire to return the favor. It says that if you get a gift, you will want to reciprocate in some way, shape, or form. In fact, the desire is to give something of even greater value to the person who gave the first gift. If you get in the trenches with your subordinates, you are giving the people you lead the impression that you are doing them a favor by helping them with their work. This in itself makes them want to return the favor. Think about it--have you ever had help from someone who was not obligated to help? If you have, you can say that you felt the desire to reciprocate. If you want someone to do for you, it is best if you do for them first.

For leadership this means that we must find ways to give to the person we want to lead. For example, let us say that we want someone to dig a hole. If we want to make sure they dig the hole, we could use the law of reciprocation by getting in the hole and digging with them. This is very effective and allows the follower to see that you are in the mud with them digging away. Here you can also set the pace and get them to work harder than normal by working hard with them in the beginning. In just a moment you will see what I am talking about with respect to commitment and consistency.

Reciprocation also works well with compliments. A compliment is a gift, which also causes the receiver to have a desire to pay back. In fact, there are many gifts that we can give that will make employees work harder for you. You must become creative and find ways to give to them to arouse the desire in them to give back to you. In his book How to Win Friends and Influence People, Dale Carnegie talks a great deal about the ability to influence others. It is imperative, according to Carnegie, that we make the gifts sincere.

The law of commitment and consistency is a very powerful tool of influence and leadership. It was found that a person who placed a bet on a horse had the greatest confidence of the horse winning after the ticket was purchased. Another example is when you make a stock purchase. You will be most committed to the purchase after you make it, because you want to justify that purchase. Why is this? This is an internal need that says we have a desire to be consistent with what we have already done. Another way to see this is when a person takes a stand. The person will encounter personal and interpersonal pressures to behave consistently and stay committed to their initial stance. This is why it is so difficult to change someone else's beliefs, ideas, and opinions. This is the exact reason why most self-help programs fail. If a person holds a committed belief, you can never change that belief for the person by telling them what to do. If you want them to change, you have to guide them into making the decision themselves. Once they do, they will be committed and the change will occur.

This is seen in the example of someone trying to quit smoking. If someone tells them to do it, they do not want to, because they did not take the stance and decide themselves, so instead they are committed to the decision to smoke. When the person decides on their own to quit, then they own that decision and quitting is much more likely.

For leadership this says that for anyone to complete a task it is best if the task is their own task. An effective leader can create ownership of a task by asking the subordinate what they think is needed to complete the job. If their way is safe and effective, then go with it. Tell them they're doing a good job and send them on their way to do the task, and chances are the task will be completed with flying colors. Getting others to decide on what to do and how to do it is far more effective in terms of completing goals and is far more effective than telling someone what to do and how to do it. Give the person a chance to take ownership by asking for their opinion on what to do and how to do it.

With the example of getting in the trenches, this only has to happen once in a while due to the law of consistency. If, for example, you want to dig ten holes, it would be best to ask the subordinate how to dig them. This gets the employee to own the job, because it is their decision on how to complete the task. After this is done, get to work with the employee and try to set a pace that gets the employee working above their normal rate. Dig two or three holes and see what happens. Because the employee will want to maintain consistency, they will work at the pace you set. Since the employee made the decision on how to proceed, they feel committed to completing the task and you will have your holes. This works with any task, whether it is manual labor or other types of work.

This holds true for personal leadership as well. If you work the Pillars of Excellence and come up with the outcomes you desire, you will be committed to attain those outcomes. If you set the pace above your normal working pace, you will feel the need to be consistent. In fact, this is one of the reasons we develop habits. We feel the need to remain consistent, and if you have set the standards and pace higher than normal, you will want to continue at that pace. This is why we continue to exercise once we have formed the habit. We may feel bad if we do not exercise, because we are not being consistent. In fact, if you go to the gym and perform at a given intensity for a period of time, and then one day you go to the gym and reduce the intensity of your workout because you were tired, you will not feel as good as if you put forth the normal intensity.

Our bodies know the pace we set in our work, and with this knowledge our bodies release endorphins at that pace. If you do less, your body does not respond with the same level of endorphins. If you do work with the consistency you have been working with, then the body gives you the endorphins that make you feel good. The bottom line is this: if you maintain a consistent level of intensity and workload at whatever you do, you will feel good about the work you do. If you slack off the normal pace, you will feel bad.

The law of social proof is exemplified in the laugh tracks we hear on sitcoms and comedy shows. We all hate those ridiculous laugh tracks--you know, the ones the producers add to the show that give viewers at home the impression that a live audience is laughing. The sad truth is that we know these are fake laughs--we even hate them--but they are still used. Why? Because they work! What is being used in this case is the law of social proof, which says that we will determine the correctness of something by looking to see what others think about it. This means that if we hear the laugh in these tracks, we are then allowed to think it is funny, because others think it is funny. This law is so powerful that it even works when we hate the trigger that causes it--in this case, the laugh tracks.

With leadership the law of social proof can be employed by understanding that the majority sets the rules. Let us say that you are in charge of a group that is given the task of developing a product that needs to be out in less than one month. This project really needs two months for completion, but for some reason you must meet the deadline of one month. If you are leading this group, it would be very nice if you could handpick the group and could tell all the members that you chose them because they are fast workers. Let us also say that these members are really not that fast, and in fact, they are the slowest in the company. As long as they are not aware of this and truly believe they were chosen because of their greater abilities, the people in the group will believe they are part of the fastest workers in the company; therefore, their feeling is that they need to be like the group and meet expectations.

When work begins, the members of the group all start out in a fast pace and off they go. They will meet the expectation of what they believe to be the group's abilities, and they will work faster than normal. They will also work harder, because the expectation is that they are fast workers. In short, they will do whatever it takes to meet the expectation. However, this can also have the reverse effect. If you tell a good worker they are being chosen for a task because they have slipped and their work is suffering, they will fulfill your announced expectation of them with a poor performance.

For leaders this is important to understand: never give your subordinates the perception that they are poor performers. In fact, if your workforce has lacked performance, one of the first things you should check is the perception they have of themselves. It usually stems from the leaders having poor expectations of them. A leader may make a comment that his workers are lazy or not any good, and the employees will become what the leader says they are. If you let your employees know that you believe they are the best, they will perform their best. Try it--it will amaze you.

Social proof is very important for companies, especially in hiring employees. If you hire employees who believe the boss is out to screw them, then the majority of the employees will feel the same. This happens frequently in non-union-represented companies that purchase union-represented companies. Most companies that have unions invited the union in by treating the employees badly. If the group of employees that were hired had bad attitudes, these employees could change the feelings of the other employees that were treated well before. If the majority of the employees have a bad attitude, eventually the other employees will follow. If the majority of the employees have good attitudes, then eventually the other employees will have good attitudes as well.

I am not saying that those employees with bad attitudes are wrong--they may have good reason to feel as they do. The point is that people will behave the way they are expected to behave. Even if the employees are treated well, if they feel they are not, then the reality is that they are being treated badly. Reality is in the perception of the receiver, and whatever they believe is reality.

A good rule of thumb is to hire those people who meet our desire for overall production. If you get the majority of employees doing a certain task the way you want it done, then they will affect the ones who are not doing it correctly. Good workers can be infectious, so can bad workers. Try to place good workers in positions that can influence the greatest number of people, and you will have it made. In fact, it has been shown that workers often take on the traits and characteristics of their leaders (Goleman 2002), so put in leadership positions the kind of people you need to succeed. These leaders will infect the group, and the rest will be history.

Most people will say yes to those they like, even if the request is not something the person would normally do. This is the law of liking, which says we will do far more for those we like than we will for those we dislike. This is a very important trait of a good leader, and it is something that needs to be looked at closely. If you want to be a good leader, you have to influence others to do tasks to get results. Your chances of getting the tasks done are much better if you are well liked.

One important part of leadership is to get people to do things they normally would not do. If you are liked and you request a task of an employee, they will probably perform the task. For example, if you need an employee to stay late and they were planning to leave to play golf, they will be more likely to stay if they like you than if they do not like you. Build up the liking from others by doing for them and really being genuine.

This is a difficult trait to learn, but it can be learned if you are very committed to doing so. One way to get others to like you is to do things for them that show you really care. You may proclaim that safety is your number one concern for your employees, but you can't just say it--you have to show it by being truly concerned for their safety.

Physical attractiveness has been linked to being liked. Social scientists call it the halo effect. This occurs when one positive characteristic of a person dominates the way that person is viewed by others, and research shows that physical attractiveness is one of these characteristics. In most cases people have a fair amount of control over their physical characteristics. For example, being in good physical condition is an appealing physical trait. So is dressing nicely. The point is that you do have the ability to control this trait, and if you want to be an effective leader, you should get good exercise and eat right to enhance your physical appearance. You should also dress in fashion. If you dress nicely, it also raises your confidence, as does being in shape. When you take care of yourself physically, you increase the chances that people will listen to you.

Another way to improve your likeability is by similarity. People like people who are similar to them. It is very important for leaders to get on the level of their subordinates by letting them know they are no different than you. In other words, show those you lead that you are no different than them and that the only difference is in your job titles. Make sure they know their job is as important as your job.

Giving compliments that are sincere also allows you to be well liked. Tell people what they like to hear, such as how well they look or how well they performed. The best way to compliment is to give feedback that provides positive feelings. Tell others how they look as long as it is appropriate. Try to give ten compliments a day for the next ten days. This will feel uncomfortable at first, but you will very quickly get the hang of it, and you will actually enjoy the feeling you get doing this exercise.

Stephen Covey talks of this in The 7 Habits of Highly Effective People. He calls such compliments "emotional deposits" and likens the process to banking. We can either build up our emotional bank account by giving emotional deposits regularly, or we can tear it down and end up with a negative balance, where we begin to lose the ability to communicate with others because of flaky behavior.

Make it a point to give sincere emotional deposits in all of your relationships so that you can maintain a positive balance in your account.

Another way to become liked is to call someone by his or her name. Your name is the most important word in the world to you. Remembering someone's name tells the person that you cared enough to remember it. They like that, and in turn they will like you for putting forth the effort to remember and use it. It is also important to try to remember facts about what the person likes and dislikes. They love it when you mention things about their family, about their hobbies, or anything about their desires.

Giving is another way to be liked. Not just giving material things, but also giving emotional support, knowledge, advice (as long as it doesn't make them look dumb), and one of the most powerful gifts--the gift of love. I am not talking about romantic love or family love like you have for your kids; I am talking about affinity for the person. This brings me to the most effective way to be liked, and that is through communication.

There are three main aspects of communication that lead two or more people to connect. The first is that of affinity, the second is reality, and the third is communication. Affinity is defined as liking or loving a thing or person. Reality is defined as understanding between two or more parties. Communication is defined as passing a particle or thought from one terminal to another terminal or terminals.

In order for effective communication to occur, you must have affinity for the other person or persons with whom you want to communicate. Without affinity you have no communication or reality. To communicate effectively, you must also have reality with another person, persons, or thing. Without reality you have no communication or affinity. Without communication you have no affinity or reality. The point is, for there to be communication, there must be both affinity and reality. The three aspects are all dependent on one another, and if one is missing, you will fail at communication.

Effective communication is vital for the success of any leader, so it is imperative to be in affinity, reality, and communication with everyone involved with your post. This even includes you. If you do not have affinity for yourself, you will have no reality or communication with yourself. If you have no reality with yourself, you will have no affinity or communication with yourself. If you are out of communication with yourself, you will have no affinity or reality with yourself. This is one reason why it is so important to have personal leadership if you want to be an effective leader of others.

Like yourself and get others to like you. This is a very important part of leadership; if you are without it, you will lose. When you like yourself, you are more likely to do better things for yourself such as exercise, learn, and perform other growing processes like the Pillars of Excellence programs. Also, if you are liked by others, they are more likely to do what you ask, even if it is something they normally would not like to do. The bottom line is this: if you are liked, you are more influential, and when you have the power to move others, you have the power to get things done.

Now let's discuss the law of authority. Many of us have experienced the authority of a controlling boss. How many times have you willingly done something for that boss? I would bet if you are like most people you did what you were told, but you were not particularly motivated to do more than asked. One of the most powerful tools for anyone is to always do more than is expected. This is very effective, because it shows you take ownership in all you do, and you are more likely to get the promotions you desire. In fact, I live by the motto that says I will expect more from myself than anyone else could ever expect of me. I rarely experience authoritative leaders, because my motto does not allow them to bark orders at me--the work is already done. Still, we must understand the law of authority with regard to influence so that we can develop greater leadership skills, since we sometimes have to use authority to get the work done. The trick is to do this with as little damage as possible so we still get the respect we need to lead successfully.

Authority often influences simply because of expectations. For example, a police officer has the ability to gain the respect of others because of the authority he or she holds. Not often, but sometimes police abuse their authority and try to massage their ego. Uniforms are often used to portray authority, not only in police work, but in others areas as well, such as pilots, doctors, and even at your local country club, where status comes by way of a club sports coat. Whatever the uniform, authority is perceived, and this perception depends on experience. The law of authority basically says that we are more likely to do whatever we are asked to do as long as the person doing the asking holds a position of authority.

An example of this is an experiment where students were asked to participate in a study they were told was in relation to learning. The students were supposed to administer shocks for wrong answers to questions they would ask a person sitting in what appeared to be an electrical execution chair. The respondents were not real subjects, and the shock was not a real shock. The students who gave the questions and the shocks to wrong answers were not in the loop and thought they were giving the respondents actual shocks that were registered at 400 volts. The respondents would scream and kick and beg the students to stop, but the students kept giving the shock for wrong answers. Why did they continue to go to extremes and hurt their fellow man? They did this because the person directing the study held a position of authority, so they did what they were told to do. People literally remove themselves emotionally from situations like this, as we saw with Hitler, Stalin, Charles Manson, and many other murderers who told their followers what to do. These followers did whatever they were told, even if they had never done such terrible things to another human being.

Authority can get people to do some pretty horrible things, and in the end they have no sense of guilt, because in their justification they were only following orders. The person literally justifies their actions by saying it was their job to follow the order, no matter what the order was. In the case of the students giving electrical shocks to respondents, the follower of authority will even give life-taking levels of shocks just to follow orders. The followers were given orders to administer higher and higher levels of punishment. They were even told the level that would kill the person, yet they continually went on giving shocks above that level.

This experiment shows that we are willing to do to others some pretty harmful acts as long as someone with authority is telling us to do so. There can be a problem with authority, and there is a great deal of responsibility that goes in the position of authority. Often people can't handle positions of authority, because they cannot help themselves from abusing the authority. The point is this: we must be careful never to ask our subordinates to participate in unethical actions, because they will tend to follow the order if you hold authority. Authority can be a powerful tool of influence, and if used ethically it can create a very productive follower.

I do not advocate the use of authority on a regular basis, but in any organization or situation that requires some form of order there is a need for authority. For example, in aviation there needs to be one person in charge so that the airplane will be operated safely and effectively. In the case of an emergency, we do not want chaos, where there is no order for action. We need order to solve the problem and get the plane in a safe mode. The problem with this idea is that when people are being instructed by someone in authority, they often do things they normally would not do.

In several plane accidents the problem was directly associated with following a captain who took the plane into greater danger. In one case, the captain had the first officer remove a circuit breaker that provided a warning if the aircraft did not have a safe configuration for takeoff. The first officer knew that this was wrong but did it anyway. When asked why he did it, he said he felt he had to, because the captain is the boss and if he didn't he would get into trouble. The plane crashed on takeoff because they took off without the proper configuration and had no warning since the circuit breaker had been pulled.

This is common in aircraft accidents, and measures are being taken to correct the problem. One step taken is the use of crew resource management, or CRM. Pilots are being taught to work together as a team, where the crew is trained to speak up when they disagree with the captain. The training teaches the captain and the first officer to respect each other and to understand that two heads are better than one when making decisions. The goal is to try to maintain the captain's authority but to give the crew the ability to say no when appropriate. This is a very tricky situation and is often the cause of in-flight disturbances between crewmembers.

The God complex is a problem with authority in which someone who holds a great deal of power begins to abuse the power, because they feel they are never wrong. The God complex can be a problem with many professions and has been the reason for many accidents and failures of businesses. If you are a person who holds authority or who works under someone who does, it is important to do whatever you can to prevent the problems associated with authority. Using the Pillars of Excellence program will prevent the God complex, but if you are not familiar or are not yet trained on the program, make certain you understand the problems that can arise with the use of authority.

Authority can also be a friend to people and organizations with the development of leadership. When used properly, there is a sense of order because a system is in place for the proper decision-making process that allows the group to work as a team. It is important to use authority with respect and ethics. Never allow yourself to use authority for massaging your ego. Always ask yourself if what you are doing is for the issue at hand or if you are trying to push others around just to exercise your power. Remember the effect authority has and the power it holds, and remember to use it with caution.

Use authority with responsibility, and if you are the follower of another person with authority, never allow that person to persuade you to perform actions you would not do on your own. Always check your actions and make sure they are in line with your values and your code of conduct. If you are ever threatened because you will not take an action against your values, you should take the chance or quit, because if you don't you are only selling yourself out to someone else and giving them control of your life. To be a good subordinate you must be a good leader of yourself and know when to say no and when to say yes. In fact, you will never rise to the top of any organization by being a "yes employee." Instead, you will lose all respect from your superiors, and in future endeavors you will be used as a pawn, being sacrificed if something goes wrong.

I am currently working with a fellow who has been put in the position of being the fall guy. This individual was a yes man who consistently did to employees whatever he was asked to do. In fact, he says he did these things with no remorse, because it was his duty to do as his superiors asked. This came to bite him, however, because one of the people he fired sued the company and the company fired my client. This may seem unfair, as it did for him, until I showed him how giving for the sake of his boss is no better then making the decision to act unethically. We saw this with Enron and other companies that used the lower ranks to protect the upper ranks from prosecution.

Those who truly lead are those who speak and act on truth, and those who speak and act on truth lead others to do the same. Be an example to the world and always do the ethical act, even if it costs you your job. For those of you who think it is okay to screw your fellow man, remember you are only hurting yourself in the long run, because it is you who will suffer the consequences in the end. Unethical behavior will always have its consequences.

A woman I was considering for a permanent position had really summed it up. She said that it's more important to look after your own backyard even if it hurts others. She also believed it was okay to unethically use knowledge given to us in a sales meeting. A person was making a presentation to us about his marketing firm and had set out an agenda in great detail with regard to the product and service they would offer us. After leaving the meeting, the woman I was considering for permanent employment commented that she could create a marketing and advertising campaign using the materials presented to us in the meeting. She said we wouldn't have to hire him, because he had already given us everything we needed in his sales presentation.

Ethics plays a big role in business, and it surprises me how unethical people can become when they are trying to get something they want. The woman in the example above would not make a good leader, because she could not control her desire to get something for free or control her behavior, which indicated to me that she may be willing to sacrifice others for her mistakes. I could never trust someone like this. In the end, these people will always cause problems, and in some cases they may ruin a business, or even a life. Needless to say, I immediately discontinued the relationship with her, because my values wouldn't allow me to consider her recommendation and her recommendation showed a difference in our value systems.

A good leader looks out for others first, and only afterward will they give to themselves. Many people believe that in order to survive they must get as much for themselves as they can and worry about giving later. This will only land them in the poorhouse and take away all authority, because no one will ever trust them and will never do for them. It must be remembered that if you act unethically, you hurt yourself, because you know your behavior was unethical and your conscious will not let you live it down. We need others to survive, and those who follow this philosophy will be the ones who have everything and more.

The law of scarcity says that if something is rare or becoming rare, it holds greater value. Bill Phillips, the man who created the Body for Life program, was a master at this principle. He could sell anything using this simple law. I remember I would get so concerned that his products were going to be gone that I needed not only to purchase the products he advertised, but I would have to stock up on them as well. The scarcity law is a very powerful tool in sales, and it can be just as powerful in leadership.

Leadership requires the influence of others to do what needs to be done. If money grew on trees, we would not be so inclined to work very hard, because we would only need to go out and pick what we needed from the tree to get what we want. The problem is that money does not grow on trees, and for this reason we are forced to work and perform duties we sometimes would never do on our own time. Money is scarce, or should I say that it is perceived as scarce.

It is important for leaders to understand motivation from the standpoint of purpose and rewards. If we give a reward, like money, for a job well done, we want to make sure that the reward is valued by the receiver. Remember that the law of scarcity says that if something is becoming rare or is already rare, it becomes more valuable. This is why you pay just enough to please the person who is motivated by money. A stronger influence is rewards. Yes, this can cause others to give their heart and soul if the reward is of value to them. For a reward to have value it must be rare, so when we give rewards to others, we must make certain that the reward holds its value.

To hold the value of a reward one must not give it out at random. There must be set parameters to receive the reward for it to maintain its power. Sometimes the reward can be a simple compliment or a special award of some sort. The object of the game is to make the reward or award mean something to the person we are trying to motivate. If we give too big of an award or reward, we run the risk of de-motivating the person. If the reward or award is too small, we may not give them enough reason to follow through.

I am big on ethics, which is an important part of leading others using rewards and awards. We should be careful not to ruin someone by giving them too much, where the prize loses its value and the only thing that will come out of it is a person who never regains their motivation because the rewards or awards they have received can never be met again. This is why we should try to prize other people's accomplishments with nonmonetary gains. Southwest Airlines is a perfect example of an organization that uses awards and rewards effectively. They pay their employees well below industry standards, but they have the happiest and most loyal workforce out there.

The reward that Southwest gives is not even a thing; rather, it is a feeling one gets working for the company. Southwest employees are proud of their jobs, and they are proud to be a part of the company. The company's culture is one of pride and one that emanates the idea of family. You feel as though you are part of something special working for the company, and this is why culture is so important. The idea of scarcity comes in because very few companies operate this way, so the employees value their jobs. Go to other companies in the industry, and you will find that it is rare to see the value that is placed on the job. The reason for this is because some companies do not value their employees. Take, for example, one airline head who said he would rather put pop machines in the planes than flight attendants. This is a statement that says, "I don't like you, and I will do whatever I can to get rid of you." The employees at this airline do not like their jobs. In fact, the company I am talking about has a higher number of sick calls and other cost problems due to employee behavior than other organizations that show respect to employees. Southwest, on the other hand, has the lowest number of sick calls of all companies in the industry.

Good leaders show that they value scarcity by getting their employees to understand how rare the job is and how rare the culture is. They get their subordinates to want to come to work because they feel like they are valued, but they also get the employee to know the importance of doing the job the way the company wants them to do the job. Some companies believe they can get by with buying a man's back only. They are sadly mistaken. If you want anyone to perform at Optimum, it is imperative that you appeal to their heart as well. I know some people feel that the only way to get someone to do anything is by using threats. This is a very ignorant philosophy. The employees will literally do things to hurt the company because of the way they are treated. I am not saying this is correct either. I believe if you take a job, no matter what, you should do what you are expected to do; if you don't like it, you should quit. What I am saying is that leaders need to recognize how they influence the relationship, and it is often their job to swallow that bitter pill and begin to treat people within their company as assets and not as liabilities.

Of course scarcity does not always work, and for this reason it is good to know when it works the best. In a study that used cookies to show how scarcity worked, the experimenter gave half the participants cookies from a jar containing ten cookies, while the other half were given cookies from a jar containing two cookies. Those who received cookies from the jar containing two cookies rated the cookies higher than those who got their cookies from the jar with ten cookies. In short, when scarcity exists we tend to increase the quality of the scarce item. From this experiment two other findings were made. The first was that the power of scarcity was stronger when the cookies had an immediate drop in number than the ones whose numbers had already been low. In short, the cookies that rapidly disappeared had greater value placed on them. The cookies that slowly disappeared had lower ratings. In other words, we value those things that have recently become scarce than those that have been always scarce.

How does this apply to leadership? Social scientists have found that scarcity that occurs rapidly leads to turmoil and violence. We would naturally think turmoil happens to those who are already in scarcity, but the truth is that turmoil happens when the taste of the better life has been reduced. With this in mind, a leader should never up the rewards or awards to subordinates to the point that a reduction is likely to be seen, or a rapid reduction at least. Keep the rewards and awards at a level that can be maintained and slightly increased, but never decreased.

Another important finding in the cookie study showed that social demand plays a big role. If the reduction of cookies happened because of demand, then the value of the cookie was placed higher than cookies reduced for other reasons. In other words, social demand has a significant influence on the value of something that has been reduced because of demand. For the leader this is important because he or she can use social demand to excite fellow workers. For example, it is imperative to make the rewards and awards valued among all subordinates so that more and more people will work harder to get the prize for fear that someone else will beat them to it. This also says that rewards and awards should have a limit to them.

You see this when real estate companies offer trips for the highest sellers. They also use awards like the million-dollar club, where you are given recognition if you sell a million dollars worth of real estate in a year. This plan motivates people in two ways: first, the fear of pain, since they may not be a part of the winning team, and second, the pleasure of being a part of the winning team. I would be very careful with this type of award system, since it could backfire. You could end up with unethical behavior, because for some people the pain is so great that they may do anything to avoid it, or the pleasure is so great that they will do anything to get it. Scarcity has to be just right for this to work, so before you try such an idea make sure you know how to use it.

Leadership is a very responsible position that requires a great deal of knowledge about human behavior. To be a good leader requires the ability to influence your fellow man in ways that can create problems and ways that can hurt others. However, if used effectively and ethically, influence can be the most powerful tool in your leadership kit.

I want to also touch on leadership and character. To be a good leader, one's character must respect both living and nonliving entities. Steven Covey called it "principled-centered leadership," which basically means that we must adhere to principles and maintain the integrity of those principles. The problem with this form of leadership is the dynamics of principles within cultures. Years ago, for example, principles said it was okay to demean woman. For some cultures today this is still true. Character, on the other hand, says you will always behave according to your beliefs, and if your beliefs hold to natural law, you will always find yourself leading with success. In order to have good character, your character follows natural law, and for this reason I call it "character-centered leadership." I know it is a small critique, but it can mean a great deal in many situations if you are not careful.

The important point to remember is to always make your actions correspond with your words. In short, do as you say so that you become an example to others, because this is the strongest form of leadership there is. It is the most powerful form of influence around. Remember that people do not like to be told what to do, so the best way to get them to do something is to allow them to make the decision to do it. The best way to do that is to be an example of who you want them to be, or at least how you want them to behave.

To lead others all one needs to do is make known to everyone involved the goals, purposes, and action plan for the desired outcome. Then get all of those people involved in the process by making them a part of the development of the project. This can be done by getting them involved in defining and developing the goals, purposes, and actions necessary to carry out the project. In short, allow all involved to take ownership by allowing them to be a part of the planning process. It is also beneficial to give the subordinates the latitude to choose how they will do the work. As long as they know the desired outcome, how they get there is their business, as long as they stay within policy.

I would like to go into greater detail on the GPA Goal technology, because I think it is very effective for leading yourself and leading others. Really all one is doing in any leadership position is trying to accomplish a goal that has been set. This is the main purpose of leadership, and one must understand how to attain goals if they want to lead others to attain the goal at hand.

Many of us have set goals or resolutions that we never even tried to accomplish. If we did take action, it often was short-lived or not sufficient to gain the results we were after. Why do we fail to achieve our desired outcomes? There are several answers to this question, but the one that is most often the reason is that we never really wanted the goal in the first place. In fact, many of our goals are set because of the influence of others. Remember that if you want to attain anything, it has to come from you--it has to be your idea. If we set the goals we desire, then we own them; however, if we accept the goals of others, those goals actually belong to those who wanted the goal for us. You must want the goal for yourself, and this is what a good leader of the masses provides--they get you to desire the goals as they desire them. In short, they make their goals your goals.

Many times we set goals that we want, but we never define why we want the goal. In order to attain anything, we must know why we want it. Ask yourself, What is the purpose of attaining this goal? Then define it thoroughly. This is very important, because it gives you the motivation to continue when the newness wears off or when the chips are down. Knowing the purpose of our goals gives us reason to fulfill our desires and drives us to succeed. Many people set a goal with a specific purpose, but never remind themselves why they want the goal, which makes the desire fade. This means that we need to review the goals we set and the purposes for attaining those goals, which we can do using the GPA Life Cycle. This was discussed in the chapter on the Emotional Pillar, where you learned about developing the ability to manage your emotional states. It is important to attach emotion to your goals, and this is enhanced if we have a true purpose.

With goals we need to excite ourselves to attain the outcome and develop ways to maintain that excitement using purpose. A great way to develop a purpose and to remember the purpose is in developing a purpose statement. Get your emotions into the statement, and write as much as you can as to why you need to attain the goal. Getting emotion into the statement gives you the ability to take thought and turn it into action and therefore create outcome.

Another reason many people never attain the goals they desire is because they don't consistently take action to do so. Sometimes we take action, but the action is short-lived because we forgot why we wanted the goal. The action we take should be calculated action and not just massive random action. Research the best possible ways to attain the goal and follow them. In fact, this is where the Mental Pillar comes into play, where you can learn, question, test, innovate, and create new and more effective ways to attain the outcome you desire.

The GPA of the GPA Goal-Setting technology represents goals, purposes, and action. This gets you into personal leadership, and now you are ready for leading others. Since we know the formula to attain our visions, we can use this formula to help others attain their visions as well. We often hear the phrase "take ownership," which sounds like a good idea, but how do we take ownership? Ownership is a state that requires the feeling of being involved. It is about being an important part of the process in whatever we are doing. No one likes to be told what to do, but they will do it if they feel they told themselves they need to do it. This is done when you allow everyone to be involved in the process of determining outcomes. It does not take much and is a great way to get others excited about any project.

The next step is to instill purpose for attaining the desire in those who are going to work to get the outcome. This is difficult, but again if you get them involved in the creation of a purpose statement, they will feel the purpose as part of them, and in turn they will take ownership of the purpose. When you develop and write the purpose statement, get as much into the statement as you can. Tell everyone involved to get their emotions into the statement by telling them it is theirs as well. The more emotion you can get into it, the greater effect it will have. Remember, thought with emotion equals action, which leads to outcome.

Make sure everyone gets involved and excited about the project. Get everyone to give their ideas to the project, and sincerely accept their ideas as long as they reflect good ideas. Never fake liking an idea, and critique it honestly. It is your job as a leader to ask the right questions to pull the answers from your subordinates. You should take the role of a coach, not a traditional leader, because coaching allows the person to feel important and not like a piece of equipment that does what it is told. As a coach, you guide the process and allow the group to develop and create the project. The greatest benefit in this approach is not only the personal growth you will experience, but the growth of everyone involved. When people work together successfully, there is a great deal to learn from the process.

Next you need to guide the group in developing the actions required to attain the goal. Again, you will be a coach, not a dictator. You are actually allowing the group to make decisions as to the best course of action. Get everyone to come up with action ideas so they can take ownership of the plan. You can do this by making sure each member of the group is heard and that their ideas are respected. If you develop the plan yourself, others won't necessarily be excited about your ideas. Give group members the support they need by facilitating the process, not taking control of it. Let the group develop, innovate, and create an action plan that is effective in attaining the outcome. They will own it, so they will be more willing to work it consistently.

As a leader you will have a great deal of influence, and this can be seen in the cultures of companies. Companies often take on the personality of the leadership. Don't be afraid to make a fool of yourself or to make mistakes, because this allows everyone involved to know you are human. Get into the actions with passion, and you will be amazed at what people will do as long as the leader of the group is doing it. Look at members of cults and similar groups-- they will even go to the extreme of killing themselves for the leader if he claims he intends to do so himself. This brings us to a very important point about leadership. As a leader, you hold a great deal of responsibility, and you need to be certain you maintain a very ethical base so that no harm is done to others. Always work to improve the lives of others, and never do anything that would hurt the human aspect of the group.

Leadership requires a great deal of evaluation of not only those involved, but also of the progress being made with respect to the goals, purposes, and actions of the group. This should be done consistently, and a great way to track your progress personally or professionally is to use statistics and graphs. This provides a visual image of the situation and allows everyone to see it clearly. In fact, these statistics and graphs should be placed where everyone can see them and where they will see them frequently. Once you know the condition of any progress, you should openly assign that area a condition. These conditions can be created by the group, or you can use the following generic conditions.

You can have a condition where nothing is happening. In this case, the progress is null and everything is stagnant. Next you could have a condition of growth, where you see a slight increase on the graph. You could also have a negative condition, where the graph is showing a decline in progress. To review we have: a condition of stagnation, a condition of growth, and a condition of decline. You can also apply these to determine the condition in your personal pillars or the roles you play, just as organizations use statistics and graphs.

With statistics and graphs you will know how you are doing or how the company is doing. From here you must have a way to change any condition that is less then Optimum. Here we will consider the condition of stagnation a negative, since anything that is not growing is dying. The following are steps to correct or to promote conditions you have determined exist in any given area. For stagnation we want to remember we are in a negative state and will use a formula that is similar to what we would use for the condition of decline. The formula for stagnation:

1. Understand what you are supposed to be doing. Go back and make sure you are following the action steps that are required to attain the outcome.
2. Promote: Make sure all activities that are supposed to get done are done.
3. Produce the results needed to move forward.
4. Evaluate.

The formula for growth:
1. Economize: Here you are doing well, and you need to make sure everything possible is being done to save for the rainy day. This is a prevention step in that you are preparing for downtrends.
2. Promote: Use whatever is left to promote. If you have done all you can to prevent future downtrends, or have at least set up for dealing with downtrends, begin promotion and try to continue the rise of the statistic.
3. Evaluate.

The formula for decline:
1. Promote: Many would want to economize, but this will only make it worse. You have to get yourself or the group to produce so that you can move back to a rise on the graph. If you do not get a product out, for example, you will never get to sell it, so you will not get the money to make money. In other words, you have to spend money to make money. For an example using the Physical Pillar, if your doctor said you were on the verge of obesity, you would want to get on an exercise and nutrition program. You waited too long to do something about your weight condition, and now you are on the decline. Economizing--for example, by eliminating certain foods from your diet--would not do you too much good in this instance. You need to get all of the activities going that are necessary in order to return to good health.
2. Next you want to change the current operating base. In other words, you want to correct the cause by looking into what you

were doing wrong and changing the way you were doing it to a more effective approach.

3. Economize: Anything left over can be put in the bank, so to speak. Once you have done all you can to correct the problem, start working to get prepared for another decline.

4. Evaluate.

These steps are general in nature, but they give you an idea of what you should do in order to promote positive conditions. A good leader always knows where they are at in any moment. In aviation they call this "position awareness." You know what condition you are in at all times, and in the case of groups, you let the group know where they are at all times by using statistics and graphs. You also have the tools to change conditions that are less than Optimum. The Pillars of Excellence can help both you and your company develop position awareness. It gives you the ability to know what needs to be considered and the ability to evaluate the situation and apply the proper formulas to fix negative conditions and increase positive conditions.

There is a great deal of leadership theory here, but what I've suggested enables you to use a practical approach to leadership. It is tailored to the individual and the organization, since organizations are made up of people. The organizations that succeed are those that have the greatest number of self-leaders. They allow their members to take ownership instead of trying to control it all in a micromanagement fashion. If you lead your life by knowing what it is you want, the purpose for attaining your desire, and developing an action plan that you follow, you will be able to lead the masses. An organization that allows those who are self-leaders to lead will create an environment that facilitates the true abilities of its workforce.

Today workers are literally held back and are rarely given the opportunity to use their potential. This eliminates a large productive part of the organization, which creates a condition of decline or potential decline. However, if you allow your people to shine by giving them the ability to use their potential, the success of your company can only increase. It is important to note that for those who lead the masses, being a good coach will allow you to guide your employees instead of controlling them. The people who facilitate the true potential of themselves or others will enjoy life to its fullest and reach that ever so tough to reach pinnacle--Optimum.

CHAPTER 10

LIFE ENHANCEMENT TECHNOLOGIES

I decided to add this chapter in order to leave you with something extra you can use to help promote peak performance and the ability to manage the change. Failure is often a result of the inability to maintain pace with the change of a growing entity. I have developed a peak performance tool and management tool that will allow you to successfully navigate your desires and manage them effectively.

The technology I created is called the GPA Life Enhancement technology. These tools use the GPA philosophy described throughout the book. To make sure you understand these powerful tools, I want to provide you with a little more detail for greater understanding. The GPA Life Enhancement technology consists of three tools: the GPA Goal-Setting technology, the GPA Life Cycle, and the GPA Life Management system. In fact, the GPA Life Enhancement technology is a step-by-step formula in which each technology provides the necessary tools to complete any task, and the three GPA technologies offer a system that gives you the ability to attain goals, to develop extraordinary drive, and a way to schedule the process.

With personal and professional leadership we must know where we are going, why we are going there, and how we will get there. We can do this with the GPA Goal-Setting technology. The great thing about this technology is that it can also be used in all of our activities from setting life-long goals or even if we are going to visit a friend. It pertains to everything we do, and when you have learned and practiced this technology, you can greatly increase your chances of getting what you want.

The GPA Goal-Setting technology allows you to know exactly what you want, why you want it, and how you can get it. Remember, the initials GPA in the GPA technology stand for Goal, Purpose, and Action. If we want to attain anything, we must ask ourselves three questions: What do I want? Why do I want it? How can I get it? You must know exactly what it is you want. This must be very clear and you should be able to see the goal in your mind's eye. Next you should know why you want the goal; in other words, you need to define your purpose for attaining the goal. Get as much emotion into the purpose and define it clearly. The last question that you need to address is how to attain the goal or what actions must be taken to achieve the goal.

Often we set goals in such a way that they are simply dreams. They have no emotion attached to them. The GPA Goal-Setting technology allows you to move the goal to a "must" level. We may say something like, "I want to be wealthy." But this is not clear. You must define what it means to be "wealthy" if you are ever going to attain wealth. For example, you can say I want to attain a net worth of one million dollars. This is a clear and concrete goal, and you know exactly what you want.

Another reason many people never attain the goals they are after is because the goal lacks meaning. Goals may have meaning when we initially set them, but after a while the pain we experienced falls off and we forget why we set the goal in the first place. We must be clear about the purpose, and the best way to do this is to describe in detail why you want the goal. For example, if your goal is to attain one million dollars, then you must know why you want the money. You can't just say, "Because I want to be rich." It must be deeper than that. Maybe you want it because you want to provide your kids with a financially secure environment. You may also want financial peace. The point is to come up with as many reasons why you want it and get them clearly defined. It is important to note that all goals are primarily a desire to attain a certain emotional tone. For example, if your goal is to lose body fat, the real motivation is not the loss of the body fat. Rather, it is how you will feel when you reach your desired body fat level. This may be the sense of an accomplishment, greater self-confidence, or attaining higher levels of energy. The point is this, when we give purpose to our goal, it is the feeling we are after that motivates us.

The last step to attaining goals is to develop an action plan. This is where many people fail in attaining their desires. You must develop an action plan that will provide you with a clear, step-by-step plan that will take you to the desired outcome. It is important at this point to take consistent action. To take action consistently we need to have a driving force that will keep us focused. The GPA Goal-Setting technology has built into it the ability to do just that. First, it allows you to know exactly the goal you are after. Then it gives you the ability to fuel your action with a clear, defined purpose, and finally you will be driven to take action using the GPA Life Cycle.

With personal or interpersonal leadership we must maintain a focus on our desired outcome, and a great way to do this is using the GPA Life Cycle, where you review the goals, purposes, and actions every day in a heightened emotional state. This is best done during exercise like a jog or a brisk walk, going over in your head or on note cards your goals, purposes, and actions, which will help to internalize them. Keep in mind that internalizing is not just memorizing; it is feeling them as if they are real. This is also a great time to visualize the outcomes as if they actually have occurred. The idea is to say them with emotion and strength. When you use the GPA Life Cycle, you literally internalize your goals, purposes, and actions. When you use physiological and psychological techniques that the GPA Life Cycle provides, you open up your subconscious due to heightened emotional states, which bring pleasure in attaining the goal you desire.

The GPA Life Management system can help you manage your life in such a way that it takes into account your goals, purposes, and actions. It is a time-management tool and a life-planning tool all in one. Many schedulers allow a place for you to schedule meetings and appointments, providing you with a task page and a contact page. These tools work to some extent, but they are not at all effective at the level needed to live a life of fulfillment. The GPA Life Management system allows you to schedule your goals in such a way that you are given the opportunity to provide fuel and an action plan that can be scheduled months in advance.

The nice thing about the GPA Life Management system is that it can be used with any planner or even just a piece of paper. We are currently in the process of developing the GPA Life Management Planner, which will be available soon, but again, you don't need to purchase this to experience the system's effectiveness. The process is very simple. First you define the goals you are after. As discussed in the GPA Goal-Setting technology, make sure these goals are defined in a clear way with as much detail as you can. The next step is to define the purpose for attaining that goal, making sure you apply emotion in your definition. It's important to note that the GPA Life Cycle and the GPA Life Management system are interchangeable.

It doesn't really matter which one you do first; however, doing the GPA Life Cycle allows you the opportunity to internalize the material. Finally, you create the action plan. The effectiveness of this tool is that you are consistently looking at and scheduling the goals, purposes, and actions together. You don't have to go to separate pages, which makes it more efficient. The system also forces you to consistently work with your goals, purposes, and actions. Once you have internalized your goal, purpose, and action using the GPA Life Cycle, you'll be able to develop a schedule using the GPA Life Management system with clarity and consistency.

The GPA Life Enhancement technology is a fantastic tool that will guide you to attain any goal you are after. The simplicity of it is that it allows you to set goals, define purposes, and develop action plans that can easily be remembered in a step-by-step fashion. Here's an example to show you exactly how this would be done.

Let's say you want to lose weight and get into shape. This is the typical extent of the goal that somebody may set. They may write it down in their planner and develop a plan of action, but it is done in such a way that the action steps are not taken consistently. To turn this goal into reality, we simply use the GPA Life Enhancement system in the following manner.

Your first step is to perform the GPA Goal-Setting technology. Here, you'll take the goal and define it in detail. In the example above your goal is to lose weight and get into shape. This goal is not defined well enough, however, and should be defined in more detail. You want to get into the picture the exact amount of weight you want to lose--in fact, the exact amount of fat you would like to lose. You also would like to define what it means to you to be "in shape."

A well-defined goal may look like this: I want to lose ten pounds of body fat and have a body fat level of 8 percent. With regard to being in shape I would like to be able to run three miles in under thirty minutes and have a resting heart rate of sixty beats a minute. You may also add to this by saying: I want my blood pressure to be at 120/60. Now you have a well-defined goal that includes the attainment of 8 percent body fat, running three miles in under thirty minutes, and having a blood pressure of 120/60.

The next step is to define the purpose or the reason why you want to attain this goal. Again, you need to get more detail into the picture. Remember, state the emotion or feelings you are trying to achieve. For example, you may say that losing 8 percent of body fat, running three miles in under thirty minutes, and having a blood pressure of 120/60 will provide you the opportunity to see your kids grow and allow you to get to know your grandchildren. It may also mean that you now get to enjoy life because you'll be more active. You'll be able to live a longer life of higher quality and enjoy your success with vitality.

The last step is to develop an action plan that will take you to your desired goal. If you're not familiar with health and fitness, you may need to do some research or hire a personal trainer. This would be part of your action plan. Assuming that you do understand health and fitness and what needs to be done, your action plan may look something like this: Assess my current condition by measuring my body fat, running three miles and timing it, and taking my blood pressure. From there your plan would have you exercise three times a week on Monday, Wednesday, and Friday performing anaerobic exercise. You may exercise aerobically three times a week on Tuesday, Thursday, and Saturday. You may say that you'll stretch every single day. You'll develop the actual diet you'll be on; in this case you may say: I will eat six Zone meals a day that include one-third protein, one-third carbohydrates, and one-third fat. You'll also take your blood pressure on a regular basis, so you will set a day each week to do so.

The action plan will look something like this on paper:
Anaerobic exercise three times a week: Mon., Wed., Fri.
Aerobic exercise three times a week: Tues., Thurs., Sat.
Stretch every day
Eat at three-hour intervals six Zone meals
Take blood pressure every Saturday

There you have it, the action plan that can be used to attain the goal you desire. The great thing about this is you know exactly what you're after, why you want it, and how you will get there.

The next step is to create your GPA Life Cycle. This will include movement and reviewing all of your goals, purposes, and actions. For example, you may wake up in the morning, throw on your gym clothes, and go outside for a brisk walk. During your walk you'll review your goals in detail, review your purposes in detail, and review the action plan that you have set, including the actions you'll take that day. This allows you to focus on what it is you want and get emotion into the picture. Back in the Emotional Pillar chapter we talked about using your physiology and your psychology to change state. Performing the GPA Life Cycle also allows you to raise your emotional state to a higher level so that your day will start off on a high note.

Once a week you can put together your GPA Life Management system and schedule your activities at least one week out. I like to schedule my goals, purposes, and actions from the date I start toward the attainment of the goal to the target attainment date. This allows me to focus on what is important--and that is action. If you do it this way, all you have to do is focus on the action. If you apply these steps, I guarantee success.

The GPA Life Enhancement technology is a wonderful tool in all activities no matter what you are doing. If you are going to visit a friend, ask yourself, What is the goal or the outcome I want from this visit? and remember to get as much detail into the picture as possible. Then ask yourself, Why do I want to get this outcome? And finally ask yourself, What do I have to do in order to attain this outcome? I highly suggest that you use visualization and see your goals, purposes, and actions clearly on a regular basis. In your GPA Life Cycle this should be part of your activities. Get your picture clear and visualize the success and how you will feel when you attain the goal.

One more point I need to make very clear is that goals can be elusive for several reasons. One reason is because we often look at the goal in a wrong way. In the example above, we stated that the goal is to attain 8 percent body fat, run three miles in under thirty minutes, and attain a blood pressure of 120/60. This is a goal; however, it is only a secondary goal to what you are really after--and that is the feeling you'll get when you attain this goal. Get into your picture the emotion you are after, and try to actually feel it as if you have already attained it.

In conclusion, start using the GPA Life Enhancement system consistently in all of your activities, and you will begin to realize how effective it really is. To become good at anything you have to practice it, and using this system consistently will allow you to become good at applying the system to all areas of your life. Use it in your Spiritual, Physical, Mental, Emotional, Social, Service, and Leadership Pillars. Also, use it as much as you can in the roles you play, and you will begin to see how effective it is in all areas of your life. Remember, teaching the system will help you internalize it, so teach it to others whenever you can. This will not only help you learn the system, but it will also allow you to contribute to others as well.

CHAPTER 11

CONCLUSION

Now that you've read about the Pillars of Excellence program, it is important to use what you have learned. Make sure you cover all areas, including your Spiritual, Physical, Mental, Emotional, Social, Service, and Leadership Pillars, so that you can experience the life you have always dreamed of. Also apply what you have learned in the roles you play. In short, put the system together in all areas of your life and enjoy the growth you will experience.

By using the GPA Life Enhancement technology, you'll be able to attain all of your desires. Teach what you have learned to someone else so that you can internalize it and help them attain the goals they want. There are many personal development programs out there--peak performance programs and others--that will help you attain the goals you want. I honestly believe that the Pillars of Excellence and the GPA technologies are some of the most powerful tools you can use, because they take into account real research that has been proven. I love to hear about other people's success, so please contact me and let me know how you are doing with the program.

We have many other programs you can use in order to improve your life, and they can be found on our Web site at www. pillarsofexcellence.com. You can also call us at (513)770-0102.

I would love to talk to you personally, so I'll be happy to talk to you in a heartbeat. I also have a couple of other programs that I think will help you tremendously. They are the Pillars of Excellence Optimum Performance Coaching and the Pillars of Excellence Life Improvement Courses.

The coaching model that I have developed takes into account everything you have read in this book, and you will get professional guidance in understanding these technologies in greater depth. We use an approach that allows you to develop from inside-out, as we believe you already have the answers to life's complex problems that you face every day. We provide you guidance in finding those answers, which will allow you to develop a life that you can call Optimum. We will help you develop an extraordinary life in which you'll achieve fulfillment--guaranteed or your money back. In fact, all of our products have a money-back guarantee, because we believe in them.

The coaching model is very effective, as we provide a variety of assessment programs that can help us determine where you are. It also allows us to define your personality type, which can help us find new ways to motivate you and give you the tools to motivate yourself. We develop personalized programs from these assessments and from intake forms in which we assess with you all of your desires. We then develop your GPA for each area. We cover the Spiritual, Physical, Mental, Emotional, Social, Service and Leadership aspects. We also work in the roles you play, and help you develop those as well.

When you complete the coaching program, you will have developed a definite purpose for your life. You will set goals, purposes, and actions in all of your pillars and the roles you play. You will define your values and beliefs and eliminate limiting beliefs that may have been holding you back. In short, you will walk away from the coaching program with a life manual that will provide you with the goals, purposes, and actions needed to attain a more fulfilling life. I look forward to working with you and providing you with the newest technologies.

I am constantly looking for new ways to improve our programs. I spend a great deal of time in research and development as we put together programs that can enhance your life. One of my favorite tools is the Pillars of Excellence Life Improvement Courses. These provide continuing education in many different areas in life, including developing relationships, evaluating behaviors, communications, and much more. These courses are inexpensive, but are praised for their effectiveness. We have a total of twenty-five different courses you can choose from, so I am sure we can meet all of your needs in this department. Many of these programs can give you guidance in personal and professional development, and we have administrative technologies available for those of you who are entrepreneurs. You can order any of these programs on our Web site at www.pillarsofexcellence.com or by calling (513)770-0102.

I hope this has been a successful journey and that you have gained knowledge, wisdom, skill, and creativity. I also hope that you have made progress already and are moving toward greater success. I hope you have told others about the Pillars of Excellence program and have guided them by teaching them the skills. Go out and make a difference in this world by helping others find the life they desire. If you are interested, we also provide a coaching certification program in which you'll be guided in learning how to disseminate the Pillars of Excellence technologies to others. The program is intense and very difficult, but it's worth the effort. Many of the currently available coaching programs work, but I believe they don't work as fast as they should. In fact, many of the coaches who have certifications need more education in the area of personal development. All of our coaches are highly trained professionals, so you'll be provided with only the best professional people in the business and will gain this same professionalism, which will give you the ability to be a successful coach yourself. Contact us today for further information about these coaching programs. I also look forward to seeing you at one of our seminars or other life-changing events, where we can exchange success stories that bring all of us the joy and fulfillment we are after.

My hope is that you'll live life with purpose and drive, energy and vitality, knowledge and creativity. That you'll live life with excellence and passion, integrity and trust, contribution and character-centered leadership. I hope your life is a gem, and I hope I have been able to bring to you a way to make it better. If you are suffering from depression, or if you really want to make a difference in your life, give us a call today so you can begin to enjoy life at its fullest.

My goal is to provide you with only the best products so that I can bring to you by way of beneficence the ability to grow. Again, I thank you for giving me this opportunity to be a part of your life. Good luck, and may you always see the positive in life and share with others your desire to help.

APPENDIXES

This part of the book is to help you in creating your initial personal development program. I have provided you with some sample exercises you can do with each of your pillars that will guide you in creating the life you have always dreamed of. Take your time with the exercises--they will be very helpful.

APPENDIX 1

YOUR VALUES, BELIEFS, PURPOSE, AND LIFE STATEMENT

CLARIFYING YOUR VALUES

As mentioned in the Spiritual Pillar, knowing your values will give you greater knowledge of self. One way to develop your values is through questions. Ask yourself the following question in each pillar and in each role you play:

What is most important to me spiritually?
What is most important to me physically?
What is most important to me mentally?
What is most important to me emotionally?
What is most important to me socially?
What is most important to me as a servant?
What is most important to me as a leader?

In each role you play, do the same thing. For example:

What is most important to me as a husband/wife?
What is most important to me as a brother/sister?
What is most important to me professionally?

You will probably find many things that are important to you. List them and try to find the one that represents you the best. This is a great exercise, because it allows you to really get to know who you are and what you value. Many times we are totally unaware of what we value, so this exercise will allow you to identify your own values and get rid of values those that may have been pushed on you.

Give this exercise your best effort. I suggest that you do repeat the exercise often, at least once a year, to get a better understanding of yourself and to keep track of your values. Have fun with it! As a reminder, we offer individual coaching, group coaching, and many coaching techniques that will guide you in developing your values.

Identifying Your Beliefs

The next exercise will help you identify your beliefs. Beliefs have the ability to move us forward or hold us back, and it is crucial that you recognize your beliefs if you want to attain peak performance in all you do. The questions below will guide you in evaluating your beliefs, eliminating those that hold you back and creating empowering beliefs that support your growth.

To find your beliefs ask yourself the following:

Limiting Beliefs:

What do I believe is holding me back spiritually?
What do I believe is holding me back physically?
What do I believe is holding me back mentally?
What do I believe is holding me back emotionally?
What do I believe is holding me back socially?
What do I believe is holding me back in service?
What do I believe is holding me back as a leader?

Then ask yourself the same question in terms of the roles you play. For example: What do I believe is holding me back as a husband/wife, as a father/mother, as a professional? Make sure you are looking internally, not externally, for your answers. In other words, you do not want to include those things you feel are holding you back externally. We have the power to overcome any obstacle outside of us as long as we empower ourselves internally.

EMPOWERING BELIEFS:

What do I believe I am spiritually capable of?
What do I believe I am physically capable of?
What do I believe I am mentally capable of?
What do I believe I am emotionally capable of?
What do I believe I am socially capable of?
What do I believe I can contribute?
What do I believe I am capable of as a leader?

Next ask yourself the same question in terms of your many roles. For example: What do I believe I am capable of as a husband/wife, as a father/mother, as a professional?

Once you honestly answer the above questions, you will have completed a very important exercise that will help you in awesome ways. You will know yourself better, and you will create a foundation for the code you will develop later. There are many more benefits-- too many to mention here--but I think you get the picture.

IDENTIFYING YOUR PURPOSE

Next you want to begin looking for your purpose in life. This is an exercise best done over a period of time. I will give you the basic idea, and from there you can develop it at your pace, or you can contact us to sign up for our powerful personal/professional coaching program that will guide you through the whole process. You can reach us at www.pillarsofexcellence.com or (513)770-0102.

Ask yourself the following questions:
What have I had to overcome?
What am I good at?
What do others say I am good at?
Would I perform this activity for little or no pay?

DEVELOPING A LIFE STATEMENT

Another way to find your purpose is to design a life statement. This means creating a statement that defines what you want your life to be about. Start with simple statements that describe your desires. These are "I want" statements. For example: I want people to be happy! Or I want kids to laugh! I want to help others overcome cancer! Continue with these and when you are finished, you will have a good idea of what direction you want to go.

Take what you came up with in the "I want" statements, and condense it down to one statement. Defining your purpose takes time and a great deal of thought. Take your time with this exercise, and really open up for your purpose to become very clear. Purpose gives meaning to your life, and it provides you the needed anticipation to enjoy life to its fullest.

APPENDIX 2

TOOLS FOR THE PHYSICAL PILLAR

This appendix provides you with some tools you can use in the Physical Pillar to help you get in the best shape of your life. I first want to point out that the Pillars of Excellence offers a purification program. This program allows you to rid your body of all the toxins that you ingest everyday. However, since it requires a great deal of information, it has been created separately as one of the Pillars of Excellence Life Improvement courses. If you would like to order the Pillars of Excellence Purification program, you can order it from our Web site at www.pillarsofexcellence.com, or call us at (513)770-0102.

Included here are a sample workout schedule, including anaerobic and aerobic exercise and stretching. Use these tools, and as you get better in this area, begin to develop your own plan. I believe that we learn best when we are most involved; for this reason, try to gather as much knowledge as you can in this and other areas that are a big part of your life.

SAMPLE WORKOUT SCHEDULE

Workout 1	Workout 2	Workout 3	Workout 4	Workout 5	Workout 6
Shoulders	Aerobics	Quads	Aerobics	Chest	Aerobics
Biceps	Abs	Hams	Abs	Lats	Abs
Triceps	Neck	Forearms	Neck	Erectors	Neck
Traps	Stretch	Calves	Stretch	Rear Delts	Stretch

AUTHORIZED FOOD LIST

Protein	Carbohydrates	Vegetables	Fats
Turkey breast	Fat free yogurt	Green beans	Flax seed oil
Lean ground turkey	Strawberries	Green peppers	Olive oil
Chicken breast	Orange	Mushrooms	(monounsaturated)
Orange roughy	Melon	Broccoli	FATS SHOULD
Salmon	Apple	Cauliflower	BE CONSUMED
Crab	Corn	Lettuce	USING THE
Tuna	Barley	Spinach	PRODUCT
Haddock	Oatmeal	Tomato	LABEL USUALLY
Swordfish	Beans	Onion	1 TBSP (NOT A
Lobster	Steamed wild rice	Brussels sprouts	PALM SIZE)
Shrimp	Steamed brown rice	Cabbage	
Top sirloin steak	Pumpkin	Celery	
Top round steak	Squash	Artichoke	
Lean ham	Baked potato	Cucumber	
Buffalo	Yam	Zucchini	
Egg whites	Sweet potato	Asparagus	
Low fat cottage cheese		Peas	

Eat 3 meals a day choosing a palm-size portion of one item from the protein, carbohydrate, and vegetable columns. With regard to vegetables, two palm-size servings may be used. For the 2 to 3 remaining meals choose a quality meal-replacement powder. Total meals per day should equal 4 to 6. Please follow the instructions you have been prescribed.

NOTE: A SERVING SIZE OF LIQUID FAT (MONOUNSATURATED) IS NORMALLY 1 TBSP. BE CAUTIOUS WITH SERVING SIZE. READ LABELS.

Below is an example of healthy eating for one day:

6:00 a.m.	4 egg whites, melon, spinach
9:00 a.m.	Meal-replacement powder (MRP) 1 tablespoon of flax seed oil
Noon	Turkey breast, melon, green beans
3:00 p.m.	Cottage cheese, apple, broccoli
6:00 p.m.	Chicken breast, steamed brown rice, asparagus
9:00 p.m.	Meal-replacement powder (MRP) with 1 tablespoon of flax seed oil

Remember, use olive oil when you cook!

APPENDIX 3

SAMPLE PEG LIST FOR MEMORY DEVELOPMENT

Included here is a sample peg list for your memory development. I have also added some study tips for you to use in all of your learning. We also offer a Life Improvement Course, the Pillars of Excellence study technology, which is very effective in developing your learning abilities. This is a very useful technology that can be used with both adults and kids, and I recommend you get the course. You can obtain this course at www.pillarsofexcellence.com or by calling (513)770-0102.

0=zoo
1=toe
2=know
3-mow
4=row
5=lie
6=chew
7=go
8=flow
9=boo

Here are some study tips to use immediately:

- Never go past a undefined word.
- Learn at your own pace.
- Understand all material before moving on.
- Use what you learn consistently.
- Innovate knowledge you learn.
- Create your own knowledge.

APPENDIX 4

DEVELOPING YOUR EMOTIONAL TONE SCALE

Here you will find an exercise that will assist you in developing your emotional intelligence by guiding you through the development of an emotional tone scale. This scale will allow you to evaluate your emotional tones and the tones of others. It will give you the opportunity to manage your states more effectively, and it will help you in mirroring other people's emotions so that you can help them manage their states.

It is very important to know what emotions you experience on a regular basis and to know the triggers that cause those emotions. The purpose here is to develop the emotions that put you in a peak state and to get rid of the emotions that bring you down.

We will begin by having you define your own emotional tone scale. In the Emotional Pillar chapter I used an example tone scale, which you may feel free to use, but I highly recommend that you create your own emotional tone scale, because it will help you internalize your own tones. To do this, ask yourself the following questions: What emotion is the lowest emotion I want to avoid? What emotion is a peak emotion I want to experience on a regular basis? Make a list and number it from 0 to 10. At the 0 position put the emotion you most want to avoid. At the 10 position put the emotion you most want to experience. From there, fill in the rest of the positions, 2 through 9, by gradually making the emotions more positive as you go up the scale. At about midpoint the emotions should begin to reflect a more positive tone.

For your convenience, I have included below the example I used in the Emotional Pillar. Use it as a guide, but make sure you are defining your own tone levels:

0 Despair
1 Hopelessness
2 Anger
3 Anxiety
4 Boredom
5 Mild interest
6 Strong interest
7 Enthusiasm
8 Eagerness
9 Passion
10 Serenity

APPENDIX 5

DEVELOPING YOUR CODE OF CONDUCT

In this exercise you are going to develop your personal code of conduct. Knowing your code allows you to be consistent in action, because it provides you with a point of reference regarding what you value.

To develop your code, you must first recognize your values. Consistency creates integrity, and creating a code of conduct gives you the foundation to develop true integrity. Your code of conduct basically says, "This is who I am." It is a document that gives you guidance in making decisions and in all activities that require your participation.

Put all your values in front of you and begin the process by writing "I will maintain" statements. For example, the Physical Pillar you might write: I will maintain my health and fitness. Do this for all the pillars, beginning with the Spiritual Pillar.

Once this is complete, you can turn your words into a paragraph, or leave it like it is, or continue to develop it. You will know when it is complete--it will feel good and it will inspire you.

APPENDIX 6

IDENTIFYING THE GIFTS YOU HAVE TO OFFER

In creating the contribution of your life all you need to do is ask yourself, What is most important to me in life? Here is where you want to volunteer your time, money, knowledge, or whatever else you have to give, because it will give you the fuel to contribute consistently and abundantly. Often our contribution is what gives our life meaning, and it also can create the driving force to continue. Remember the story about the woman who started MADD? If you don't, go back to the Service Pillar chapter and read it to be reminded of the power meaning has.

Again find something meaningful, but make sure the gift you give provides the receiver with the opportunity to grow as well. I believe that the person doing the giving gains the greatest benefit. For this reason, push to try to give more than you receive, and you will not only attain more, but in the end you will also be of better help to the receiver. Keep in mind that it is impossible to give more than it is to receive. The more you give, the more you get.

APPENDIX 7

ESTABLISHING YOUR OWN GOALS, PURPOSES, AND ACTIONS

I have put here some tools to help you create your goals and attain those goals. Once again, we offer many programs that support the growing process in the Pillars of Excellence Life Improvement courses and the GPA Life Enhancement courses. These programs are inexpensive, because I believe everyone should have the opportunity to gain from what they have to offer.

I only want to remind you of the GPA idea and how it is used so that you can use it in each pillar and role you play. Remember what GPA stands for? G = goal, P = purpose, and A = Action. In all of your pillars and roles, ask yourself these three questions:

1. What do I want from this pillar/role?
2. Why do I want it?
3. What needs to be done to get it?

These are three simple but powerful questions that will guide you in all your activities. Go back and look at the GPA Life Enhancement technologies--the GPA Life Management technology, the GPA Life Cycle, and the GPA Goal-Setting technology--to get a good understanding of these powerful tools. For more information on all the programs we offer, visit www.pillarsofexcellence.com or call (513)770-0102 to speak with one of our client care professionals who can help you find the best solutions for your personal development.

BIBLIOGRAPHY

Aamodt, M. G. 2004. Applied Industrial/Organizational
Psychology, 4th ed. Belmont, CA: Thomson/Wadsworth.

Baltes, P. B., and Kliegl, R. 1992. "Further testing of limits
of cognitive plasticity: negative age differences in a
mnemonic skill are robust." Developmental Psychology 28:
121-25.

Cerella, J., and Hale, S. 1994. "The rise and fall in information-
processing rates over the life span." Acta Psychologica 86:
109-97.

Cialdini, Robert B. 2001. Influence: Science and Practice, 4th ed.
Boston: Allyn and Bacon.

Covey, S. R. 2003. Focus: Achieving Your Highest Priorities. New
York: Franklin Covey.

Cowan, N., Wood, N. L., Nugent, L. D., and Treisman, M. 1997.
"There are two word-length effects in verbal short-term
memory: Opposed effects on duration and complexity."
Psychological Science 8: 290-95.

Druckman, D., and Bjork, R. A., eds. 1991. In the Mind's Eye:
Enhancing Human Performance. Washington, DC: National
Academy Press.

Fahey, J., Santos, G. 2002. "Memory improvement and research
related to the science of memory." Education 123(2):380.

Frankl, V. E. 1963. <u>Man's Search for Meaning: An Introduction to Logotherapy.</u> Boston: Beacon Press.

Giles, H., Coupland, N., Coupland, J., Williams, A. and Nussbaum, J. 1992. "Intergenerational talk and communication with older people." <u>International Journal of Aging and Human Development</u> 34: 271-97.

Gordon, T. 1977. <u>Leader Effectiveness Training; L.E.T.: the No-Lose Way to Release the Productive Potential of People.</u> New York: Wyden Books.

Greider, K. 1996. "Making our minds last a lifetime." <u>Psychology Today</u> 29(6):42. Available at http://cms.psychologytoday.com/articles/pto-19961201-000028.html.

Hertzog, C., Dixon, R. A., and Hultsch, D. F. 1990. "Relationships between metamemory, memory predictions, and memory task performance in adults." <u>Psychology and Aging</u> 5(2): 215-27.

Hollenbeck, J. R., Moon, H., Ellis, A. P., West, B. J., Ilgen, D. R., Sheppard, L., Porter, C. O., and Wagner, J. A. 2002. "Structural contingency theory and individual differences: examination of external and internal person-team fit." Journal of Applied Psychology 87(3):599-606. Available at <u>http://www.ncbi.nlm.nih.gov/entrez/query.fcgi?cmd=Retrieve&db=PubMed&list_uids=12090618&dopt=Abstract</u>.

Hultsch, D. F., and Dixon, R. A. 1990. "Learning and memory in aging." In J. E. Birren and K. W. Schaie, eds. <u>Handbook of the Psychology of Aging,</u> 3rd ed. San Diego: Academic Press.

Kark, R., Shamir, R., Chen, G. 2003. "The two faces on transformational leadership: dependence and empowerment." Journal of Applied Psychology 88(2):246-

55. Retrieved 10/17/2003, from Academic Search Premier.

Kausler, D. H. 1985. "Episodic memory: memorizing performance." In N. Charness, ed. Aging in Human Performance. New York: Wiley.

Kirkpatrick, S. A., and Locke, E. A. 1996. "Direct and indirect effects of three core charismatic leadership components on performance and attitudes." Journal of Applied Psychology 81(1):36-51.

Langer, E. 1989. Mindfulness. Reading, MA: Addison-Wesley.

Lorayne, H., and Lucas J. 1974. The Memory Book. New York: Stein and Day.

Lorayne, H. 1990. How to Develop a Super-Power Memory. Hollywood, FL: Fell.

Lorayne, H. 1990. Super Memory--Super Student: How to Raise Your Grades in 30 Days. Boston: Little, Brown.

Lorayne, H. 1995. Secrets of Mind Power, 1st ed. Hollywood, FL: Lifetime Books.

McConnell, J.V. 1962. "Memory transfer through cannibalism in planarians." Journal of Neuropsychiatry 3 (Supple. 1):542-48.

Miller, G. A. 1956. "The magical number seven, plus or minus two: some limits on our capacity for processing information." Psychological Review 63: 81-97.

Myerson, J., Hale, S., Wagstaff, D., Poon, L. W., and Smith, G. A. 1990. "The information-loss model: a mathematical theory of age related cognitive slowing." Psychological Review 97: 475-87.

Nairne, J. S., Neath, I., and Serra, M. 1997. "Proactive interference plays a role in the word length effect." Psychonomic Bulletin and Review 4: 541-45.

Reber, A. S., and Reber, E. 2001. The Penguin Dictionary of Psychology, 3rd ed. New York: Penguin.

Robbins, S. P. 2003. Essentials of Organizational Behavior, 7th ed. Upper Saddle River, NJ: Prentice Hall.

Salthouse, T. A., and Babcock, R. L. 1991. "Decomposing adult age differences in working memory." Developmental Psychology 27: 763-76.

Selye, H. 1985. The Stress of Life, 2nd ed. New York: McGraw Hill.

Shimamura, A. P., Berry, J. M., Mangels, J. A., Rusting, C. L., and Jurica, P. J. 1995. "Memory and cognitive abilities in university professors: evidence for successful aging." Psychological Science 6: 271-77.

Simonton, D. K. 1990. "Creativity and wisdom in aging." In J. E. Biren and K. W. Schair, eds. Handbook of the Psychology of Aging. San Diego: Academic Press.

Thompson, L., Aranda, E., Robbins, S. P. 2000. Tools for Teams: Building Effective Teams in the Workplace. Boston: Pearson Custom.

Weiten, W. 2002. Psychology: Themes and Variations; Briefer Version, 5th ed. Belmont, CA: Wadsworth/Thomson.

Yates, F. A. 1999. The Art of Memory. London: Routledge and Kegan Paul.

Yukl, G. 2002. Leadership in Organizations, 5th ed. Upper Saddle River, NJ: Prentice Hall.

ABOUT THE AUTHOR

A professional athlete in two national sports leagues, a certified pilot and flight instructor, a health and fitness guru, a respected scholar, and now a renowned Optimum Performance Coach, Dr. John P. DeMann is truly a modern day Renaissance Man in every sense of the word.

Through his own life enhancement strategies John has achieved more than many others could hope for in several lifetimes. John has also recognized, through his own experience, and scholarly research that helping others to achieve the same level of performance has resulted in greater personal fulfillment and a clear mission that he centers his life around. Also, a passionate orator and one of today's great creative minds, John's seminars have been described by many as a "life changing experience."

Please consider John's personal invitation to join him, and many others, as you learn about the empowering strength we all have inside us, through the Pillars of Excellence program.

Printed in the United States
103156LV00006B/194/A

9 781425 939083